The Paleo Cookbook for Kids

The Paleo Cookbook for Kids

83 FAMILY-FRIENDLY PALEO DIET RECIPES FOR GLUTEN FREE KIDS

SALINAS PRESS

Contents

Introduction

What is the Paleo diet? It's a way of eating that emphasizes real food and natural flavors, colors, and textures. It has become the gold standard for a healthful, balanced diet. It is based on following the diet that humans consumed for millennia before the invention of agriculture, when grains and legumes began to take center stage. Looking at the decline in human health since that time, one could argue that as a species, humans were meant to eat fruits and vegetables, nuts, and meats—not grains and legumes.

The goal of this book is to help you serve kid-friendly Paleo meals to your children throughout the day. Part One introduces the foods, equipment, and techniques for your Paleo kitchen; Part Two offers a range of recipes for meals, snacks, and sweets, with special emphasis on lunch.

Your child may be on the Paleo diet for any of the same reasons that an adult is: better health and vitality, better digestion, fewer toxins, reduced allergies and inflammation, better and more restful sleep, clearer skin, and healthier hair. A Paleo diet is also associated with improved glucose tolerance, so it may be helpful for children and adults with diabetes. Sustained weight loss and improved mood are two more benefits of this diet. And while there are other benefits that could be listed, there is no corresponding list of disadvantages to a Paleo diet for you and your children.

At first, your children may wonder why their peanut butter sandwiches, pizzas, and tacos have disappeared. You can help them understand by pointing out two basic facts: First, foods like peanut butter sandwiches are now just pale versions of their former selves, since the original ingredients are virtually stripped of nutrients and fiber. Second, the primary ingredients used to make that sandwich—grains and legumes—are difficult for us to digest and in some cases can even make us sick. Of course, understanding why something is not all it should be is not the same as replacing a yearning for a pizza or a sandwich. This book offers attractive substitutions for comfort foods your kids might miss.

If your kids ask why a Paleo diet is good for them, the grocery store provides a good lesson in its benefits—one your kids can't help but notice. Point out the fresh foods arranged around the perimeter of the store. Produce and meats don't have labels with a list of ingredients. All you need to know about those foods is contained in their names: apple, chicken, egg. Now travel down the cereal or cracker aisle and look at any package. The ingredient list will be long and likely full of items that have four or more syllables. These additives and derivatives aren't real foods; in fact, they are called "food ingredients" to distinguish them from a more "natural" version of the original food.

Cooking Paleo for your children is an exercise in abundance. Fruits and vegetables offer more colors and look delicious because they are so bright and vivid (most processed foods fall within a short beige color spectrum). Nor does Paleo cooking mean that you must spend hours at the stove. In fact, it could liberate you from the stove, since many foods are ready to serve without any cooking at all.

You may wonder how you will fill plates and stomachs without mashed potatoes or spaghetti. Filling a plate with salads, raw vegetables, and fruits makes the plate look enticing and will tempt your children to try a bite. Soon the unfamiliar becomes familiar and potentially a new favorite.

Some children are introduced to a whole new world of foods when they start a Paleo diet. It can feel unfamiliar at first. Overcoming resistance to foods or textures or flavors is a simple matter of being patient and persistent. While you are making the transition, it might make sense to stick to familiar foods that get a good reception, even if that means serving the same basic menu for several days or weeks in a row. Adding new flavors and recipes slowly is a good way to break the old routine little by little. A great place to start is by offering your own version of beloved dishes from a favorite ethnic restaurant.

Use the information you find in Chapter One and the sample menu plan in Chapter Two to get your kids involved in planning meals. Everyone likes to have some control over what they will and won't eat; it's human nature. The food lists in Part One, as well as lists from online sources, will provide you with plenty of inspiration. The recipes in Part Two will show you the best way to begin: Tasting a new food in small amounts is the optimal way to introduce a new flavor. Children are often willing to taste "one forkful," so it's a good strategy to assemble plates that offer a little bite of a lot of things.

The main thing to remember—and to tell your children—is that the Paleo diet means your options are pretty much wide open, as long as the foods you consume are as whole, unrefined, and unprocessed as possible. If one food doesn't pass the kid taste test, you can be sure something else will.

You know there will be times when you face challenges. The best way to head off those situations is to meet them head-on with your own alternatives. Breakfast cereals can still be something crunchy in a bowl with cold milk, and you can still offer fruit, pancakes, or even waffles. Lunch can still include sandwiches, wraps, tortillas, burgers—even pizza. You can still enjoy baked goods like brownies and chocolate chips to satisfy an urge, or crunchy chips and crackers to scoop up dips.

When your children are on their own, you have to rely on them to make their own good choices. The foods you buy, the meals you make, and the answers you give to their questions can build a strong foundation. Paleo kids get the best of all possible worlds: plenty of foods that make them strong and keep them healthy, and parents who care enough to feed them well and teach them why food matters.

PART ONE

The Paleo Diet

CHAPTER ONE

Getting Kids Started on the Paleo Diet

Keeping your children Paleo at breakfast and dinner is a simple task, but when you send them to school the story changes. The typical school lunch is hardly Paleo friendly. Your Paleolithic forbearers would not have been carrying peanut butter and jelly sandwiches, bags of chips, and cookies in little brown bags.

Finding new options for those traditional lunches can be a shared project for you and your children. You get to explore a bigger and brighter universe of foods and flavors at every meal. Lunches made from fresh, whole foods are brighter, more bountiful and colorful, and more fun to eat than a boring PB&J any day.

A kid's Paleo lunch can have plenty of healthful foods with a rich assortment of all the major nutrients, whether you are new to Paleo or an old hand. It just takes a little planning to make the foods you are already preparing for your family perform double duty as lunches, but this is a routine part of feeding a family, no matter what that family eats.

This book is about more than lunch, of course. The day begins with a nourishing breakfast, and you'll find choices here that start the day with protein-packed dishes. Dinner is also important because you'll be able to parlay those dinners into lunches later in the week. Paleo kids need snacks and desserts too, and you'll find plenty of recipes made from honest ingredients that make the most of the flavors and textures kids love. Putting it all together in a weekly plan makes shopping and cooking easier, and Chapter Two takes a look at menu planning and shopping strategies.

FOODS TO ENJOY

What can you put in your child's lunch box? There's a pretty big list to choose from that includes meats, eggs, fruits, vegetables, nuts, seeds, and even some sweets. Kids following a Paleo diet can eat the same foods that you do. Begin by looking over the lists below to find the foods you and your children enjoy. These lists don't include every possible option. If some of your favorite foods don't appear here, you can find additional resources in the Appendix (page 145) that will help you find even more Paleo-friendly foods.

Meats

- Beef
- Buffalo/bison
- Goat
- Lamb
- Pork
- Rabbit
- Veal
- Venison

Cured Meats and Sausages

- Bacon
- Corned beef
- Ham
- Pastrami
- Prosciutto
- Salami

Fish and Shellfish

- Bass
- Bluefish
- Clams
- Cod
- Crab
- Haddock
- Hake
- Lobster
- Mackerel
- Mahimahi
- Mussels
- Oysters
- Salmon
- Shark
- Shrimp
- Trout
- Tuna

Poultry (and Eggs)

- Duck
- Emu
- Game hen
- Goose
- Ostrich
- Partridge
- Pheasant
- Turkey

Nuts*

- Almonds
- Brazil nuts
- Cashews
- Coconut
- Hazelnuts
- Macadamia nuts
- Pecans
- Pine nuts
- Pistachios
- Walnuts

*Peanuts are not included in this list because they are not nuts; they are a type of legume (bean) and therefore are excluded from the Paleo diet.

Seeds

- Chia
- Flax
- Hemp
- Poppy
- Pumpkin
- Sesame
- Sunflower

Fruits

- Apples
- Bananas
- Berries (blackberries, blueberries, cranberries, raspberries, strawberries)
- Citrus (clementine, kumquat, lemon, lime, orange, tangerine)
- Grapes (black, Concord, green, red)
- Kiwi
- Lychee
- Mango
- Melons
- Papaya
- Pears
- Pineapple
- Plums
- Star fruit

Vegetables

- Artichoke
- Asparagus
- Avocado
- Beans, green
- Broccoli
- Carrots
- Cauliflower
- Celery
- Corn
- Cucumber

- Eggplant
- Fennel
- Garlic
- Greens, leafy
- Leeks
- Onions
- Peas, green
- Peppers and chiles
- Pumpkin
- Radishes
- Shallots
- Squash, summer and winter
- Tomatoes
- Turnips
- Zucchini

Condiments and Seasonings

- Coconut aminos
- Fish sauce
- Herb and seasoning blends, salt-free
- Mustard
- Pepper
- Seed and nut pastes
- Spices
- Tamari, gluten-free
- Vinegar

Fresh Herbs

- Basil
- Bay leaves
- Chervil
- Chives
- Cilantro
- Dill
- Marjoram
- Mint
- Oregano
- Parsley
- Rosemary
- Tarragon

Beverages

- Fruit juices (if made with a juicer)

FOODS TO MODERATE OR LIMIT

Some levels of the Paleo diet do not include foods like beets and vinegar. Other levels permit limited amounts of starchy vegetables.

While most dairy, including milk and cheese, is excluded on the basis of its lactose (sugar) content as well as its casein content (which is responsible for most cow's milk allergies), some levels do include butter and cream since they are primarily butterfat, as long as it is from grass-fed cows. Still others may include aged cheeses, made from raw milk if possible.

- Dairy (including milk, cultured milk, whey, cheeses, cream)
- Butter or cream, grass-fed
- Salty foods (chips, crackers, French fries)
- Vegetables with starch content (beets, potatoes, sweet potatoes)
- Vinegar

FOODS TO AVOID

- Fruit juices (if not made with an extractor)
- Grains, especially refined and processed grains made into breads, cereals, crackers, and pasta
- Baked goods: wheat, rice, rye, barley, corn, millet, quinoa, oats, buckwheat
- Ketchup, barbecue sauce, teriyaki sauce, and hot sauces that include sugar or salt
- Legumes such as black beans, chickpeas, lentils, navy beans, peanuts, and soybeans
- Processed meats that contain nitrates (deli meats, hot dogs, and sausages)
- Soft drinks
- Sugar (white and brown, corn syrup, molasses, pancake syrup, refined honey) as an ingredient in beverages, prepared and processed foods, and desserts

IN THE PANTRY

If you've been cooking Paleo for a while, you probably have a good assortment of ingredients in your pantry, but with the exception of a few flours and cooking fats, there is relatively little that is difficult to find in any well-stocked market. Keeping your pantry stocked saves time and money. Even more important, a good pantry can be an inspiration, suggesting new flavors and combinations to spice up old favorites.

Cooking Fats and Oils

- Coconut oil
- Nut oils (almond, pistachio, walnut)
- Safflower oil
- Sesame oil (light for cooking; dark for seasoning)

Condiments

- Coconut aminos
- Mustard
- Tapenade
- Vinegar (unfiltered apple-cider vinegar or red-wine vinegar)

Flours and Meals

- Coconut flour
- Nut flours (almond, chestnut, hazelnut, pecan, walnut, pistachio, macadamia)

Canned Goods

A few canned foods are actually better for you because of the type of processing they undergo. Fermented foods like pickles and sauerkraut, made by traditional methods, have live cultures that give them significant health benefits as well as great flavor. And while canned tomatoes aren't fermented, the processing they undergo makes good-quality canned tomatoes an important food to have on hand year-round for sauces, soups, stews, and salsa when fresh tomatoes aren't in season.

- Artichokes packed in oil or brine (without added sugar or sucrose)
- Coconut milk (full-fat)
- Fish (tuna, salmon, sardines, and anchovies, oil-packed or packed in water)
- Olives
- Roasted peppers
- Tomatoes (brands without sugar or salt)

Nuts, Seeds, and Dried Fruits

Nuts are a great addition to many dishes, whether they are eaten as a snack or ground into a fine meal to make pancakes and porridge. However you intend to use them, it's best to buy nuts in the shell—or minimally processed—whenever possible. Keep nuts in the freezer and they will last for months. Look for them during the fall—nuts are seasonal—when the prices are better and the selection is bigger.

Dried fruits are also good to add to porridges, puddings, trail mix, meatballs and meatloaf, salads, and on their own as a snack. Avoid candied or crystallized fruits that have been poached in syrup and glazed with sugar, and look for sun-dried varieties that haven't been treated with sulfites.

- **Coconut:** unsweetened (chips or shredded)
- **Dried fruits:** apricots, blueberries, cherries, cranberries, currants, dates, raisins (Zante), mango, peaches, prunes
- **Nuts:** almonds, Brazil nuts, cashews, chestnuts, hazelnuts, pecans, pistachios, walnuts
- **Seeds:** flax, poppy, pumpkin, sesame, sunflower

COOKING TIPS

There aren't any special tools required, but some tools are especially helpful for certain tasks.

- Baking sheets and dishes
- Food processor and blender
- Heavy-gauge skillet for sautéing and frying; cast iron is a great choice
- Mandoline or Benriner for making slices and julienne
- Microplane, vegetable peeler, and grater for cutting vegetables
- Mixing bowls
- Mortar and pestle for grinding spices or making sauces like guacamole
- Nut grinder or spice grinder
- Roasting pan
- Sharp knives, and a sharpening stone or steel for keeping the blades sharp
- Storage containers

Lunch Containers

You can find a variety of lunch containers made in a variety of materials. Some have several compartments, like bento boxes and stacking systems. To increase the appeal of lunches, get your kids involved in selecting what to put into each compartment. They can fill them up while you are making dinner and put them in the refrigerator to chill overnight.

KID-FRIENDLY COOKING

There are plenty of ways to get kids involved in cooking. One simple but often overlooked task is setting the table. Here are some others:

- Cracking and blending eggs
- Grating vegetables on a box grater, or into ribbons with a vegetable peeler*
- Grinding or puréeing foods in a food processor or blender*
- Making roulades or rolling up grape leaves (pages 91 and 77)
- Making salads and salad dressings
- Rinsing vegetables
- Shredding meats by hand
- Tearing herbs or cutting them with scissors*

*Chores involving sharp tools or cooking on the stovetop or in the oven should be done under adult supervision.

TEN STEPS FOR A SUCCESSFUL TRANSITION TO THE PALEO DIET FOR KIDS

1. **Make one simple change at a time.**
   Be kind to them and to yourself. Make it a slow transition rather than a big shift. Drop pasta first, then cut back on breads.
2. **Make it their Paleo diet, not yours.**
   Learn about the Paleo diet and give your kids the facts. Help them to notice how foods make them feel by asking them. Once they say out loud that they feel stronger and more energized (in whatever terms they use), it becomes true.

3. **Find flavors and textures to fill up the empty holes.**

   You may not be able to replace every texture and taste, but you can find foods that are satisfying in their own right. Emphasize those foods, even if it means you have to wait to introduce a wider variety. If putting kale chips on everything with a side of Paleo ranch makes them happy, so be it for the time being.

4. **Meander toward your goal.**

   Keep your priorities in mind, but don't make it the focus of every dinner conversation, shopping trip, or menu-planning session.

5. **Let them choose.**

   Knowing in advance what you'll be cooking is good for your sanity. That's where the menu plan (Chapter Two) comes in. If you involve everyone in planning, you are far more likely to find the foods and dishes they will all enjoy. Then, menu in hand and lists at the ready, take them with you to the supermarket. Be prepared to point out all the good choices and let them choose.

6. **Set a good example.**

   Let them see you stretch your horizons by trying new combinations and flavors. And if you have a craving for something you normally don't eat, be honest. It is most effective if your honesty ends by saying something like "and so, instead of the Friday-afternoon pizza at the office, I broke out my famous trail mix and popped cauliflower." (It's even better if you can say that everyone loved them—and should that moment ever come, they will!)

7. **Don't sweat the small stuff.**

   If lunches come back partially eaten, it probably isn't meant as an insult or a complaint. Maybe they were not really hungry when it was time for lunch.

8. **Be prepared for parties.**

   Birthday parties, cookouts, picnics, and class trips can all pose a challenge. Talk to the host or hostess and offer to bring something that you know your kids will eat. Chances are the other kids will enjoy it too.

9. **Tell them to blame it all on you.**

   If the other kids wonder why your kids don't eat bread or spaghetti, let them blame it on you. Don't be surprised if your kids' lunches look much more interesting than most things put between two slices of white bread.

10. **Be consistent by being prepared.**

    Remove the foods you don't want to serve from your pantry, refrigerator, and freezer, and restock with Paleo foods that you can use to create meals, snacks, and treats in the same amount of time as it takes to get take-out pizza.

TEN STEPS TO KEEP YOUR KIDS HAPPY ON THE PALEO DIET

1. **Add more colors.**
   Add as many colors as possible to every meal.
2. **Add more shapes.**
   Cut foods into chunks, slices, slivers, and cubes—just don't make everything on the plate the same shape.
3. **Add more crunch.**
   Fresh, raw, crispy foods satisfy more than one of the senses.
4. **Try something surprising.**
   Try something new whenever you have the chance, whether it's a new combination or a new fruit.
5. **Deconstruct your favorites.**
   Take apart dishes like soups, stews, casseroles, and salads into their ingredients and enjoy each on its own.
6. **Have pancakes for dinner.**
   Or have burgers for breakfast. Do something unexpected.
7. **Travel.**
   Go to a foreign country at your dinner table so that you can learn about a new dish from another culture.
8. **Accessorize.**
   Keep your audience in mind when it comes to heat levels and spice, but don't be afraid of flavor in the form of condiments, sauces, pickles, and relishes made without added sugars or gluten.
9. **Celebrate.**
   When you feel good, you have fun. When you have fun, you feel good. Help your kids celebrate lunch by sending them off with a fun thermos or lunch bag.
10. **Splurge.**
    Eating a Paleo diet means you aren't buying expensive processed or packaged foods, so spend that money on an occasional luxury like lobster or a juicy steak.

CHAPTER TWO

A Seven-Day Paleo Meal Plan for Kids

The key to success with your kids on a Paleo diet is having a plan to follow. Shopping becomes easier, and when you are ready to cook, you have all the ingredients you need on hand. A meal plan won't stifle your creativity. In fact, it will give you more flexibility. You can adapt the meal plan in this chapter to fit your family's particular needs. For example, if you spend a lot of time at practices, games, or other events that might overlap with mealtime, you should be on the lookout for recipes that travel well or reheat easily when you can't all eat together. For more recipes, go to *The Paleo Cookbook: 300 Delicious Paleo Diet Recipes* (Rockridge Press, 2013).

USING THIS MEAL PLAN

Keeping a family's schedule organized would be difficult without a calendar and to-do lists. The same is true for meals. The calendar, in this case, is one week. You can fine-tune a week's worth of meals—simply repeat them if you like—but if you follow the basic principles of this meal plan, you can easily add variety, take advantage of seasonal specials, and try something new that sounds or looks interesting.

Know whom you will be cooking for and when.

When your children are very young, it is easy to know who will be home for meals. By the time middle school begins, chances are good that regular mealtimes may get interrupted. Keep that in mind when you select recipes for dinners.

Make leftovers part of your plan.

The idea of cooking forward, or getting two meals from one cooking session, has great benefits. Look for recipes that are easy to double and that can be refrigerated or frozen and then reheated. When you are buying meats for a dinner, buy a pound or so more than you need for that meal. You'll have ingredients ready for salads, wraps, soups, and frittatas for the next day or two.

Let the market plan some of the menu.

Whether you shop at farmers' markets or supermarkets, the produce and meats on display follow a certain sequence: When they look freshest and most appealing, they are also most flavorful and wholesome. Your menu plan can hang loose on some details—the exact cut of fish or type of leafy vegetable—so that your meals have the fullest flavor as well as a wide range of foods.

Use the meal plan to keep your pantry stocked.

When you make a weekly shopping list, you will include all the fresh and perishable items you need, but don't overlook the staple items you use regularly and should always have around. Review your recipes to identify which pantry items you are running low on that week. During certain weeks you will need a lot of onions and spinach; for others it will be olive oil and tahini.

Match the recipe to the time you have for cooking.

There may be some days when you can afford to put a dish on the stove to cook for hours; choose big roasts and braises for those days and plan subsequent meals around those dishes by making hash, burritos, salads, meatballs, or stir-fries later in the week. Look for short ingredient lists and meals that cook fast in one or two pans for your busy nights.

THE SEVEN-DAY MEAL PLAN

MONDAY		NOTES
Breakfast	Granola Fresh fruit Nut milk	
Lunch	Prosciutto-Wrapped Individual Frittatas Raw veggies Ranch Dressing or Dip Fresh fruit	
Dinner	Grilled London Broil with Chimichurri Sauce Grilled veggies	Grill extra veggies to use in lasagna on Tuesday
TUESDAY		**NOTES**
Breakfast	Sweet Potato Pancakes Eggs (fried, poached, or scrambled) Fresh fruit	Make extra pancakes to use with sliders for Wednesday lunch
Lunch	Taco Bowl Salsa Guacamole Fresh fruit	
Dinner	Lasagna Veggie salad Fresh fruit	
WEDNESDAY		**NOTES**
Breakfast	Greenie Smoothie Banana Muffin	
Lunch	Sausage Sliders Coleslaw Fresh fruit	
Dinner	Meatloaf Steamed or stir-fried veggies Green salad Triple-Berry Cobbler	

THURSDAY		NOTES
Breakfast	Pumpkin Porridge Apples	
Lunch	Roast Beef Roulades Guacamole Plantain Chips	From Wednesday dinner
Dinner	Lamb Chops with Herbed Mash Roasted veggies Ginger Apple Crisp	
FRIDAY		**NOTES**
Breakfast	Breakfast Hash Eggs (poached, fried, or scrambled) Fresh fruit	From Wednesday dinner
Lunch	Lemon Chicken Salad Roll Raw veggies Fresh fruit Sesame Crackers	From Thursday dinner
Dinner	Shepherd's Pie Green salad Chocolate Banana Pudding	Make extra for lunches next week
SATURDAY		**NOTES**
Breakfast	Breakfast Hash Fresh fruit Banana Muffins	
Lunch	Chicken Strips Coleslaw Raw veggies	
Dinner	Pulled Pork Herbed Mash Roasted veggies Fresh fruit	

SUNDAY		NOTES
Breakfast	Oven Pancakes with Berries	
Lunch	Waldorf Wrap Coleslaw Plantain Chips Fresh fruit	
Dinner	"Noodles" and Meatballs Veggie salad Fresh fruit Brownies	
SNACKS		**NOTES**
	Kale Chips "Popcorn" Chocolate Chip Cookies Granola Bars Zucchini Fries	

PART TWO

Recipes

CHAPTER THREE KID-FRIENDLY BREAKFASTS

Kid-Friendly Breakfasts

Building a healthy breakfast is the first step toward a great day for your child, whether she is off to school or off to play or practice. If you aren't already in the habit of offering a nourishing, filling breakfast, these tips will help you fit breakfast-making into busy schedules.

Plan ahead to breakfast when you are making dinner. Having some leftover vegetables or meats already cooked, cut, and ready to go makes it easy to put together a quick veggie-and-egg scramble, an omelet, or a quick hash in the morning. Make a big batch of pancakes or waffles. Freeze the extra and reheat in the toaster oven or microwave.

If breakfast isn't your child's favorite meal, you can try a few of these time-tested approaches:

- Use fresh fruit, raw honey, or maple syrup to make the "medicine" go down.
- Smoothies are easy to make (good for you) and easy to eat—good for sleepyheads or busy bees who have a hard time getting to the breakfast table on time.
- Grab-and-go options like containers of Paleo-friendly granola, fresh fruits, muffins, and burritos mean you don't have to worry about flagging energy in the middle of the morning.
- Most juices sold in supermarkets aren't a good bet, even if they aren't made from concentrates and don't list sugar in the ingredients. Make your own juices with an extractor or juicer to get all the benefits of fresh fruits and vegetables.

Greenie Smoothie

There is something fresh and invigorating about this sweet-tart smoothie made with avocado for creaminess. Make the smoothie in two batches to be sure the blender doesn't overflow.

6 STRAWBERRIES

1 ORANGE, PEELED AND SEEDED

1 AVOCADO, PEELED AND PITTED

½ CUP DICED MANGO OR PEACH (FRESH OR FROZEN)

1 CUP FILTERED WATER

4 ICE CUBES

Combine the strawberries, orange, avocado, mango, water, and ice cubes. Pour half into a blender and blend until very smooth and frothy. Pour into two glasses. Blend the second half of the smoothie, and pour into two glasses. Serve immediately.

Granola

If your children miss the breakfast cereals you're not buying anymore, you'll need a good Paleo-friendly substitute. This granola makes a great crunchy-cereal alternative topped with almond milk and sliced fresh fruit or berries. You can make large batches of this granola to have on hand for quick snacks or to add as a topping to Banana Muffins (page 31) or Sweet Potato Pancakes (page 35).

1 CUP NUT PIECES (ALMONDS, WALNUTS, PECANS, PISTACHIOS)

1 CUP UNSWEETENED SHREDDED COCONUT

½ CUP SEEDS (FLAX, SESAME, SUNFLOWER, CHIA, PUMPKIN)

½ CUP CHOPPED DRIED FRUITS (DATES, CRANBERRIES, CHERRIES, MANGO)

¼ CUP ALMOND OR SUNFLOWER SEED BUTTER

3 TABLESPOONS RAW HONEY

2 TABLESPOONS COCONUT OIL, MELTED

½ TEASPOON SEA SALT

1 TEASPOON GROUND CINNAMON

¼ TEASPOON VANILLA EXTRACT

¼ TEASPOON GROUND GINGER

1. Preheat the oven to 275°F. Line a baking sheet with parchment paper.

2. In a large bowl, combine all ingredients and toss until evenly coated. Spoon the mixture onto the prepared baking sheet, spreading it in an even layer.

3. Bake until the coconut and nuts have a rich aroma and a light color, 20 to 25 minutes. Stir the granola from time to time to brown it evenly.

4. Let the granola cool completely, then break it into chunks. Store in an airtight container at room temperature for up to 2 weeks.

Pumpkin Porridge

MAKES 4 SERVINGS

Choose a pure pumpkin purée without sweeteners or added flavoring (the label should simply say "pumpkin"). You can also use sweet potato in place of pumpkin purée. If you have pumpkin purée left over after making this porridge, you can use it in place of the sweet potato in Sweet Potato Pancakes (page 35).

1 CUP WATER

1 CUP ALMOND FLOUR

½ CUP PUMPKIN PURÉE

2 TABLESPOONS GRADE B MAPLE SYRUP

½ TEASPOON VANILLA EXTRACT

½ TEASPOON GROUND CINNAMON

PINCH OF GROUND NUTMEG

PINCH OF SEA SALT

½ CUP DICED APPLE

½ CUP CHOPPED PECANS

1. In a saucepan, stir together the water, almond flour, pumpkin purée, maple syrup, vanilla, cinnamon, nutmeg, and salt until smooth.

2. Place over medium heat and bring to a simmer, stirring frequently, until the porridge thickens, about 5 minutes.

3. Serve the porridge in heated bowls topped with the apple and pecans.

Banana Muffins

MAKES 12 MUFFINS

If you have bananas that are ripening before you are ready to make these muffins, put the bananas in the freezer with the peels on. They will fall apart into a velvety purée when they thaw.

COCONUT OIL, TO COAT THE MUFFIN TINS

½ CUP ALMOND FLOUR

¼ CUP COCONUT FLOUR

1 TABLESPOON GROUND CINNAMON

1 TEASPOON GROUND NUTMEG

¼ TEASPOON SEA SALT

3 OR 4 RIPE BANANAS

4 EGGS, ROOM TEMPERATURE

2 TEASPOONS VANILLA EXTRACT

1 TABLESPOON RAW HONEY, MELTED (OPTIONAL)

1. Preheat the oven to 350°F. Coat two muffin tins lightly with coconut oil.

2. In a bowl, whisk together the almond flour, coconut flour, cinnamon, nutmeg, and salt.

3. In a separate bowl, mash the bananas with a fork into a smooth purée. Add the eggs, vanilla, and honey.

4. Add the dry ingredients to the wet ingredients and stir to make a smooth batter. Spoon the batter into the muffin tins, filling them about three-quarters full.

5. Bake until the muffins spring back when lightly pressed in the center, 25 to 30 minutes.

6. Cool the muffins in the tins for a few minutes before turning them out onto a rack. Keep muffins at room temperature in an airtight container for up to 3 days.

Crêpes

MAKES 10 CRÊPES

You will find plenty of ways to use these thin but rich, eggy pancakes. They are pliable enough to roll around fillings, perfect to replace tortillas, and great in a Paleo-friendly lasagna. For breakfast, enjoy them simply rolled up or folded into quarters, served with fruit and some raw honey.

6 EGGS
1 CUP UNSWEETENED ALMOND MILK
2 TEASPOONS COCONUT OIL, MELTED, PLUS MORE FOR COATING PAN
3 TABLESPOONS COCONUT FLOUR, SIFTED
1 TEASPOON ARROWROOT POWDER
¼ TEASPOON SEA SALT

1. In a mixing bowl, whisk together the eggs, almond milk, and coconut oil. In a separate mixing bowl, whisk together the coconut flour, arrowroot, and sea salt.

2. Add the wet ingredients to the dry ingredients and stir together to make a smooth, relatively thin batter.

3. Heat a crêpe pan or a small sauté pan over medium-high heat and brush with coconut oil. Pour ¼ cup of the batter into the pan, tilting and swirling it to coat the pan evenly. Cook over medium heat until the edges of the crêpe begin to look dry, about 1 minute. Use a spatula to flip the crêpe and cook on the other side for 1 or 2 minutes, until done.

4. Transfer the crêpe to a platter while you finish cooking the remaining batter. Separate the crêpes with parchment paper before wrapping and storing them.

FILLINGS

ALMOND BUTTER AND SLICED PEACHES, APPLES, OR BANANAS
BERRIES WITH LEMON JUICE AND A DRIZZLE OF HONEY
SCRAMBLED EGGS, SAUSAGE, AND SAUTÉED VEGGIES
BLUEBERRY OR PEACH COMPOTE WITH CHOPPED NUTS

Oven Pancakes with Berries

MAKES 4 SERVINGS

These big, puffy pancakes are a perfect weekend treat, since the entire family will want to see the spectacular puff as each comes out of the oven. The only real difference between these and other pancakes is that these use almond flour instead of wheat flour; the eggs give the dish its spectacular lift. Try this pancake with other seasonal fruits: bananas, peaches, nectarines, pears, plums, and cherries.

2 TABLESPOONS BUTTER (PREFERABLY GRASS-FED), MELTED

1 CUP FINELY GROUND, BLANCHED ALMOND FLOUR

1 TEASPOON GROUND CINNAMON

¼ TEASPOON SEA SALT

6 EGGS

½ CAN COCONUT MILK (FULL-FAT)

2 TEASPOONS VANILLA EXTRACT

½ PINT BERRIES (BLACKBERRIES, BLUEBERRIES, RASPBERRIES, OR STRAWBERRIES)

¼ CUP GRADE B MAPLE SYRUP

1. Preheat the oven to 375°F. Lightly brush a cast-iron skillet with butter and put it in the oven to heat.

2. In a mixing bowl, combine the almond flour, cinnamon, and salt.

3. In a separate bowl, whisk the eggs, coconut milk, and vanilla until smooth.

4. Whisk the wet ingredients into the dry ingredients until just blended.

5. Pour the batter into the hot skillet and scatter the berries evenly on top. Bake until the pancake is puffed and set, 20 to 25 minutes.

6. Serve hot from the skillet topped with berries and maple syrup.

Waffles

MAKES 4 SERVINGS

You may find that these waffles are sweet enough not to need honey or syrup. Make a thick purée of fresh fruits or berries to serve on top, or add a dollop of whipped coconut cream for a special treat. To make a savory version, you can use a wide array of fillings, including meatballs, burgers, sliced meats, and plenty of fresh vegetables. For savory waffles, omit the vanilla and cinnamon.

COCONUT OIL, FOR THE WAFFLE IRON
1½ CUPS ALMOND FLOUR
½ TEASPOON BAKING SODA
½ TEASPOON GROUND CINNAMON
PINCH OF SEA SALT
2 EGGS, BEATEN
⅓ CUP COCONUT MILK (FULL-FAT)
1 TABLESPOON RAW HONEY
1 TEASPOON VANILLA EXTRACT

1. Preheat a waffle iron to medium-high and brush the iron lightly with coconut oil or other fat.

2. In a mixing bowl, whisk together the almond flour, baking soda, cinnamon, and salt.

3. In a separate mixing bowl, blend the eggs, coconut milk, honey, and vanilla until smooth.

4. Add the dry ingredients to the wet ingredients and stir to make a smooth batter.

5. Pour about ¼ cup of the batter into the center of the waffle iron; it will spread to the edges as it cooks. Close the waffle iron and let the waffle cook until it is golden, crisp, and cooked through, about 4 minutes.

6. Keep the waffles warm while you cook the remaining batter. Serve hot.

Sweet Potato Pancakes

MAKES 4 SERVINGS

Sweet potatoes paired with bananas give these pancakes a moist, cake-like consistency, making them the perfect foil for sausage or bacon. You can use them instead of buns for hot and cold sandwiches as well. The recipe doubles or even triples easily, and frozen pancakes thaw quickly at room temperature. Just toast them in a dry skillet or a toaster oven for the best flavor. Serve them on their own, with some syrup and sliced fruit, or use them to replace buns for Sausage Sliders (page 86).

2 SMALL SWEET POTATOES (ABOUT 12 OUNCES)

½ RIPE BANANA, MASHED INTO A PURÉE WITH A FORK

2 EGGS

¼ TEASPOON BAKING SODA

PINCH OF GROUND GINGER

PINCH OF SALT

COCONUT OIL OR GRASS-FED BUTTER FOR COOKING

1. Cook the sweet potatoes in the microwave until very tender, about 8 minutes. When they are cool enough to handle, remove the skin and push the flesh through a sieve or a food mill.

2. Measure out ¾ cup of the sweet-potato purée (use the remainder in other dishes or freeze for later use). In a mixing bowl, combine mashed banana, sweet potato purée, eggs, baking soda, ginger, and salt. Stir into a smooth batter.

3. Heat a griddle or cast-iron skillet over medium-high heat. Brush lightly with coconut oil. Pour about ¼ cup of the batter onto the griddle and spread it into a circle about 3 inches in diameter.

4. Cook on the first side until the edges appear dry and there are a few bubbles on the surface, about 3 minutes. Turn the pancake over and cook the other side until cooked through, 3 minutes.

5. Serve immediately.

Sweet Potato Hash Browns

MAKES 4 SERVINGS

While you are transitioning to the Paleo diet, or just to change things up a bit, you can replace some of the sweet potatoes in this recipe with white potatoes. Fingerlings and purple potatoes have that great potato flavor along with unique shapes. Serve these crisp patties with anything that calls for a cracker, including soups and stews. Top them with a poached or fried egg for a filling breakfast dish, or fry them as small patties to use in place of buns for sandwiches.

1 SWEET POTATO, CUT INTO LONG SHREDS (ABOUT 2 CUPS)
1 YELLOW ONION, CUT INTO THIN SHREDS (ABOUT 1 CUP)
PINCH OF GARLIC POWDER
PINCH OF PAPRIKA
SEA SALT
FRESHLY GROUND BLACK PEPPER
2 TABLESPOONS OLIVE OIL

1. In a mixing bowl, toss the sweet potato and onion together with garlic powder, paprika, salt, and pepper until the seasonings are evenly distributed.

2. In a cast-iron skillet over medium-high heat, heat the oil, add the sweet-potato mixture, and spread it in an even layer. Reduce the heat to medium, cover the pan, and cook for 10 minutes.

3. Remove the cover and increase the heat to medium-high. When the bottom layer is lightly browned and forms a crust, about 3 minutes, use a spatula to turn the pancake (it's fine if it doesn't turn in one whole piece, but try to keep the crust as intact as possible).

4. Continue to cook until the hash browns are golden on the other side and fully cooked, 4 or 5 minutes. Serve immediately.

Breakfast Sausage

MAKES 4 SERVINGS

Instead of making this into patties, you can cook the sausage loose, so that it breaks up into crumbles to add flavor to tomato sauce, as a topping for pizzas, or as a filling for omelets or wraps.

1 POUND GROUND PORK

1 TABLESPOON GRADE B MAPLE SYRUP

1 TEASPOON DRIED SAGE

1 TEASPOON FENNEL SEED

1 TEASPOON GARLIC POWDER

½ TEASPOON DRIED THYME

⅛ TEASPOON RED PEPPER FLAKES

PINCH OF GROUND CLOVES

¾ TEASPOON SEA SALT

½ TEASPOON FRESHLY GROUND BLACK PEPPER

1. In a mixing bowl, mix all the ingredients together with a wooden spoon or very clean hands until they are well combined. Shape into 8 patties. Keep the sausage refrigerated if you are not planning to cook it right away.

2. Heat a cast-iron skillet or a sauté pan over medium heat. Add the sausage patties and cook, turning occasionally, until cooked through and browned on both sides, about 10 minutes. Serve immediately.

Egg and Veggie Scramble

MAKES 4 SERVINGS

There is really no limit to the vegetables you can include in this scramble. Some vegetables have a lot of moisture and may require a little more cooking time to reduce the liquid.

3 TABLESPOONS OLIVE OR SAFFLOWER OIL

2 CUPS ASSORTED RAW OR COOKED VEGETABLES, SUCH AS PEPPERS, MUSHROOMS, ONIONS, CARROTS, ZUCCHINI, CELERY, OR SPINACH, CUT INTO THIN SLICES OR STRIPS

4 EGGS, BEATEN

SEA SALT

FRESHLY GROUND BLACK PEPPER

1. In a skillet, heat the oil over medium heat. Add the vegetables and cook until very hot and tender.

2. Add the eggs and cook, stirring constantly, until the eggs are set and fluffy, about 6 minutes.

3. Season with a pinch of salt and a few grinds of pepper. Serve immediately.

Eggs in a Hole

MAKES 4 SERVINGS

You may know this dish as "windowpane eggs." Toasted eggplant replaces bread for a rich and satisfying breakfast. You can make several eggplant "toasts" and freeze the extra for a quick breakfast or light supper dish.

1 EGGPLANT

½ TEASPOON SEA SALT

5 WHOLE EGGS

½ CUP FINELY GROUND NUTS OR SEEDS (WALNUTS, PECANS, PISTACHIOS, CASHEWS, OR SESAME SEEDS)

VEGETABLE OIL

FRESHLY GROUND BLACK PEPPER OR CRUSHED RED PEPPER FLAKES

1. Slice the eggplant lengthwise into ½-inch-thick slices and sprinkle with salt. Let the eggplant drain in a colander for about 20 minutes, then rinse off the salt and blot the eggplant dry. Use a biscuit cutter to cut out a circle from the center of each slice.

2. In a large shallow dish or bowl (wide enough to accommodate the eggplant slices), beat 1 egg and 1 tablespoon water together until smooth. Place the ground nuts in a separate shallow dish.

3. Dip the eggplant first in beaten egg and then in the ground nuts. Place dipped eggplant on a rack in a baking sheet. Dip eggplant "holes" as well to make open-faced sandwiches.

4. In a deep skillet over medium-high heat, heat about ¼ inch of oil. When the oil has reached about 350°F, dip one edge of a slice to test if the hot oil is ready (it should foam and bubble). Add the eggplant slices in an even layer without overlapping or touching. Cook on one side until golden and crisp, about 3 minutes. Turn once and finish cooking on the other side for another 3 minutes.

continued ▶

5. Crack an egg into the holes in the eggplant "toasts" and season with pepper. Continue frying until the eggs are fully cooked and set.

6. Accompany with fresh salsa, sliced tomatoes, avocado, or marinara sauce.

Breakfast Hash

MAKES 4 SERVINGS

Hash has always been a dish meant to turn leftover bits of roast and vegetables into a tasty and satisfying breakfast. There is nothing more perfectly Paleo than that—and nothing is more reliably appealing than a crisp and juicy hash. The keys to success are great-tasting leftovers and a heavy-gauge cast-iron skillet. Look for nitrate-free bacon and sausage to use in the hash.

4 PIECES NITRATE-FREE BACON, MINCED

1 TEASPOON OLIVE OIL

2 GARLIC CLOVES, CRUSHED

1 SWEET POTATO, CHOPPED

1 RED BELL PEPPER, CHOPPED

1 CUP CHOPPED SPINACH, KALE, OR ESCAROLE

1 TOMATO, FINELY CHOPPED

2 LINKS CHICKEN SAUSAGE, COOKED AND CHOPPED

SEA SALT

FRESHLY GROUND PEPPER

1. In a cast-iron skillet over medium heat, slowly cook bacon in order to render the fat. When the bacon is crisp, 2 to 3 minutes, lift from the pan with a slotted spoon and drain on a paper towel–lined plate.

2. Add the oil and garlic to the bacon fat and cook until the garlic is aromatic, about 30 seconds. Add the sweet potato and cook, covered, until potatoes are tender, 6 to 7 minutes. Stir the sweet potatoes occasionally and lower the heat if necessary so the potatoes don't scorch.

3. Remove the cover, increase the heat to medium-high, and add the pepper; sauté until it is hot, 2 minutes. Stir in the spinach, tomato, and sausage, and continue to cook until all the ingredients are very hot. Season with a pinch of salt and a few grinds of pepper. Serve immediately.

Beef and Kale Frittata

MAKES 4 SERVINGS

Frittatas are perfect to serve hot from the oven, warm, at room temperature, or even cold. Make this while you are preparing dinner the night before for a quick breakfast that is easy to reheat, or wrap in a slice of turkey or ham for a grab-and-go meal.

2 TABLESPOONS OLIVE OR SUNFLOWER OIL

1 YELLOW ONION, DICED (ABOUT ½ CUP)

2 SHIITAKE MUSHROOM CAPS, SLICED

6 OUNCES GRASS-FED GROUND BEEF

½ TEASPOON SMOKED PAPRIKA

¼ TEASPOON SEA SALT

½ TEASPOON FRESHLY GROUND BLACK PEPPER

2 CUPS SHREDDED KALE (OR ¾ CUP FROZEN KALE, THAWED AND
    SQUEEZED OF EXCESS MOISTURE)

8 CHERRY TOMATOES, HALVED

4 EGGS, BEATEN

1. Preheat the oven to 350°F.

2. In a cast-iron or an ovenproof nonstick skillet, heat the oil over medium-high heat. Add the onion and sauté, stirring frequently, until tender but not brown, about 3 minutes. Add the mushrooms and cook until hot.

3. Add the ground beef, paprika, salt, and pepper and sauté, stirring to break up the meat, until it is cooked through, about 4 minutes. Stir in the kale and tomatoes, and continue to cook until the kale has wilted and the tomatoes are hot, 2 to 3 minutes.

4. Pour the eggs over the meat and vegetables. Transfer the pan to the oven and bake until the eggs are fully cooked and set, about 20 minutes.

5. Let the frittata rest for 5 or 10 minutes. Cut into wedges and serve.

Breakfast "Burritos"

MAKES 4 SERVINGS

This is a satisfying, hearty breakfast that you can put together ahead of time and bake in the oven while everyone is getting dressed.

4 COLLARD GREEN LEAVES

1 TABLESPOON SAFFLOWER OR OLIVE OIL

½ YELLOW ONION, THINLY SLICED

1 GREEN BELL PEPPER, THINLY SLICED

1 RED BELL PEPPER, THINLY SLICED

1 POUND GROUND TURKEY

1 TEASPOON CHILI POWDER

½ TEASPOON GROUND CUMIN

SEA SALT

FRESHLY GROUND BLACK PEPPER

1½ CUPS DICED TOMATOES

CHOPPED FRESH PARSLEY OR CILANTRO FOR TOPPING (OPTIONAL)

1. Preheat the oven to 350°F.

2. Rinse the collard leaves and trim the stems. Set aside.

3. In a cast-iron or ovenproof nonstick skillet, heat the oil over medium-high heat. Add the onion and sauté, stirring frequently, until tender but not brown, about 3 minutes. Add the peppers and cook until tender, about 2 minutes.

4. Add the ground turkey, chili powder, cumin, salt, and pepper and sauté, stirring to break up the meat, until it is cooked through, about 4 minutes. Stir in half of the tomatoes and continue to cook until very hot and flavorful, about 3 minutes.

5. Divide the filling mixture among the collard leaves, rolling each leaf around the filling burrito-style (fold in the outer edges about 2 inches, then roll up the "burrito" from the bottom to completely enclose the filling).

continued ▶

6. Transfer to a baking dish, placing the burritos seam-side down, and top with the remaining half of the tomatoes. Scatter the herbs evenly over the burritos, if using, and bake until very hot, about 15 minutes.

7. Serve hot.

CHAPTER FOUR KID-FRIENDLY LUNCHES

Kid-Friendly Lunches

Sometimes you like variety and sometimes you like the comfort of familiar foods. Your kids are just like you, so it makes sense to have a number of favorites that are easy to put together with things you normally have in the refrigerator.

Variety is critical. Having a little bit of a lot of different flavors, colors, and textures makes food look more appealing. Everyone eats with their eyes. A variety of foods makes it easier to encourage kids to eat enough to get the right nourishment to carry them through the afternoon. Last, but not least, a variety means that you are getting a good array of nutrients by offering foods that are rich in proteins, healthy fats, and carbohydrates.

As you pack lunches, keep a supply of fresh fruits and vegetables already cut and ready to go, from cucumber spears to melon chunks. Fruits and vegetables that are naturally bite-size, like grapes and cherry tomatoes, are good choices too. Chilled vegetables like steamed snow peas, asparagus, green beans, or broccoli from last night's dinner can be tucked into almost any lunch recipe.

Will your children miss sandwiches made with conventional wheat bread when they see other kids at school tearing into theirs? You can head off the green-eyed monster by making lunches that have the flavors they love, just presented in a slightly new way.

The recipes in this chapter call on a few special skills:

Making Roulades

If your meat slices are not really big enough to make a decent-sized roulade, simply overlap two or three smaller pieces to make the roulade.

Slicing Meats

To slice meats deli-thin, make sure they are very cold. An electric slicer can be a big help here. And if you make your own roasts often, you might want to consider buying a meat slicer for your kitchen.

Holding Roulades and Wraps Closed

Use strips of vegetables (cut with a vegetable peeler) to tie the roulades shut, if you have time. You can make time by getting your kids to cut them and assemble the roulades while you are making dinner the night before.

Making Fillings

Your wraps won't be so likely to lose their filling if the filling is cut into small pieces. If too small, they lose their distinct flavors, and larger chunks can make eating more interesting. See what your children prefer and let them help you with the wraps.

Salsa

For this salsa, add whatever you happen to have around, or add fruits and vegetables such as mango, pineapple, papaya, cucumbers, avocado, jicama, carrots . . . the list goes on and on.

½ CUP DICED, SEEDED TOMATO

¼ CUP MINCED GREEN BELL PEPPER

¼ CUP THINLY SLICED GREEN ONION

½ TEASPOON MINCED JALAPEÑO (OPTIONAL)

½ TEASPOON LIME JUICE

SALT

FRESHLY GROUND PEPPER

FRESH CILANTRO LEAVES

In a bowl, combine the tomato, pepper, onion, and jalapeño (if using). Stir in the lime juice and adjust seasoning with additional lime juice, salt, and pepper. Add the cilantro and set aside to marinate for at least 20 minutes at room temperature, or if made in advance, up to 2 days in a covered container in the refrigerator.

Paleo Mayonnaise

MAKES ABOUT 1½ CUPS

This is called Paleo mayonnaise, but it differs only slightly from a traditional mayonnaise recipe. It is made with oil, eggs, mustard, and vinegar, and omits the small amount of sugar called for in some recipes. Commercially prepared mayonnaise does include sugar in some form, as well as stabilizers. This stripped-down version takes only a few minutes to prepare, even if you are making it by hand, but you can keep the prepared sauce in the refrigerator for several days. You'll find numerous uses for it as a spread, dip, or salad dressing.

1 PASTEURIZED EGG YOLK
½ TEASPOON MUSTARD POWDER
2 TEASPOONS WATER
1 TABLESPOON LEMON JUICE
1 CUP OLIVE OIL
SALT
FRESHLY GROUND BLACK PEPPER

1. In a bowl, whisk together the egg yolk, mustard powder, water, and the tablespoon of the lemon juice, or place in a blender and blend until smooth and frothy.

2. While whisking or blending, add the olive oil gradually, a few drops at a time at first and slowly increasing to a thin stream. When all of the oil is added, the mayonnaise should be thick, creamy, and ivory in color. Add additional lemon juice if desired and season with salt and pepper.

3. Use the mayonnaise immediately or as part of a dip and spread. It can be stored in a covered jar in the refrigerator for up to several days.

Flat Omelet

MAKES 1 OMELET (1 CUP OF STRIPS)

In addition to being used as a garnish in Chicken "Noodle" Soup, flat omelets, plain or seasoned, can be used as pancakes to top almost anything. Of course, you can also use a flat omelet as a wrap by filling it with meat or vegetables. Add 2 or 3 tablespoons of minced or shredded herbs, green onions, or spinach for color and flavor.

2 EGGS
SEA SALT
FRESHLY GROUND BLACK PEPPER
1 TABLESPOON OLIVE OIL

1. In a bowl, beat the eggs until well blended and season with a pinch of salt and pepper.

2. In a small skillet or omelet pan, heat the oil over medium-high heat. Pour in the eggs and let them cook until the bottom and edges are beginning to set, about 2 minutes. Push the set eggs from the edge to the middle of the pan, allowing the uncooked egg to flow to the edges. Continue cooking the eggs in this way until they are set into a large, flat omelet.

3. Using a spatula, turn the omelet over once and cook on the other side for about 30 seconds. Tip the omelet out of the pan onto a clean plate. Let it cool for a few minutes, then roll it into a cylinder and cut it crosswise into thick or thin strips as needed.

Bone Broth

Bone-based broths are an amazing source of nutrition and one of the most versatile ingredients in any kitchen, especially a Paleo kitchen. Your own broth is sure to be lower in fat and sodium than prepared broths. If you make it in large batches, it is easy to keep on hand in the refrigerator or freezer. Use it to poach or simmer meats, fish, or poultry; your reward is a doubly rich broth that you can serve on its own. Add it to vegetables for flavor, or use it to make vegetable purées that don't call for added cream or butter.

1 POUND BEEF OR VEAL KNUCKLES OR MARROW BONES

1 POUND OXTAILS

½ POUND CHICKEN NECKS OR BACKS

1 GARLIC BULB, SEPARATED INTO CLOVES AND PEELED

2 TABLESPOONS UNFILTERED APPLE CIDER VINEGAR

1 TEASPOON SEA SALT

4 QUARTS COLD FILTERED WATER, PLUS MORE AS NEEDED

1. In a stockpot, combine the bones, oxtails, chicken necks, garlic, vinegar, and salt and add enough of the cold water to cover the bones by about 2 inches.

2. Bring to a simmer and cook over low heat, skimming the surface if necessary, until the broth is very flavorful and clear.

3. Strain through a fine-mesh sieve into clean containers. The broth can be used immediately or stored in covered containers in the refrigerator for up to 1 week, or in the freezer for up to 2 months.

Chicken "Noodle" Soup

MAKES 4 SERVINGS

This recipe is made with a bone broth, a staple in the Paleo diet. It has two kinds of noodles: wide zucchini or yellow squash strips, and thin omelet strips. Feel free to add whatever vegetables are on hand for an even heartier dish.

1 QUART BONE BROTH (PAGE 52)

1½ CUPS CUBED OR SHREDDED COOKED CHICKEN

½ CUP SLICED CELERY

½ CUP SLICED CARROTS

½ CUP GREEN PEAS (FRESH OR FROZEN)

½ CUP DICED SWEET POTATO

1 CUP RIBBON-CUT ZUCCHINI OR YELLOW SQUASH (OR A COMBINATION)

1 CUP RIBBON-CUT STRIPS OF FLAT OMELET (PAGE 51)

3 TABLESPOONS CHOPPED FRESH PARSLEY

SEA SALT

FRESHLY GROUND BLACK PEPPER

1. In a soup pot over medium-high heat, bring the broth to a simmer. Add the chicken, celery, carrots, peas, and sweet potato. Simmer until the vegetables are tender and the broth has a rich flavor, about 20 minutes.

2. Add the zucchini ribbons and continue to simmer until they are limp, 3 to 4 minutes.

3. Stir in the omelet strips and parsley, and season the soup with salt and pepper.

4. Serve immediately in heated bowls, or transfer to a thermos or microwave-able container for a school lunch.

No-Bean Chili

MAKES 4 SERVINGS

While you probably won't miss the beans at all, you might want something close to cornbread for sopping up the chili. Try Sweet Potato Pancakes (page 35) for a great alternative.

If you have time to let the chili sit overnight in the refrigerator, do so; this is the kind of dish that develops more flavor and is better the next day. Just heat up portions as you need them, including to pack into thermos containers for lunch away from home.

2 TABLESPOONS OLIVE OIL

1½ POUNDS GROUND TURKEY

½ CUP CHOPPED ONIONS

1 CUP CHOPPED RED AND GREEN BELL PEPPERS

¼ CUP CHOPPED POBLANO CHILE (OPTIONAL)

2 TEASPOONS MINCED GARLIC

1 TABLESPOON CHILI POWDER

1 TEASPOON GROUND CUMIN

1 TEASPOON DRIED MEXICAN OREGANO

SEA SALT

FRESHLY GROUND BLACK PEPPER

2 TABLESPOONS TOMATO PASTE

1 CUP DICED TOMATOES

1. In a cast-iron or ovenproof nonstick skillet, heat the oil over medium-high heat.

2. Add the turkey and sauté, stirring frequently to break it up, until it is cooked through, about 8 minutes. Transfer with a slotted spoon to a plate.

3. Add the onions, peppers, chile (if using), and garlic to the skillet, and sauté, stirring frequently, until tender, about 5 minutes.

4. Add the chili powder, cumin, oregano, salt, and pepper, and stir until blended. Add the tomato paste and cook until it has a sweet aroma and turns brick red, about 2 minutes.

5. Return the turkey and any of its juices to the vegetable mixture and stir to combine. Add the diced tomatoes with their juices and bring to a simmer over medium heat until all of the ingredients are very hot and the chili is flavorful. Season with salt and pepper.

6. Serve immediately or pack in a thermos container.

Coleslaw

MAKES 3 CUPS

The combination of green and red cabbage and black poppy seeds makes this salad bright and appealing. Replacing the traditional mayonnaise dressing with a simple vinaigrette gives it a bright flavor that kids love.

1 CUP SHREDDED SAVOY CABBAGE
1 CUP SHREDDED RED CABBAGE
½ CUP SHREDDED CARROTS
½ CUP SHREDDED CELERY
2 TABLESPOONS OLIVE OIL
1 TABLESPOON LEMON JUICE
1 TEASPOON POPPY SEEDS (OPTIONAL)
SEA SALT
FRESHLY GROUND BLACK PEPPER

1. In a large bowl combine the savoy and red cabbage, carrots, and celery and toss to mix.

2. In a small bowl whisk together the oil, lemon juice, and poppy seeds (if using).

3. Pour the vinaigrette over the cabbage mixture and toss to coat evenly. Season with salt and pepper. Serve immediately or store in the refrigerator in a covered container.

BLT Salad

The T *in* BLT *stands for turkey as well as tomato, but there is plenty more in this eye-catching, satisfying salad. Look for nitrate-free bacon; if it is not available in your local markets, see the Appendix (page 145) for substitutions. For even more protein, add a few wedges of hard-boiled egg or a sprinkle of nuts. This makes a great lunch for a crowd too. You can build it in a big salad bowl or platter.*

1 CUP SHREDDED ROMAINE

½ CUP CUBED OR SHREDDED TURKEY

3 TO 4 AVOCADO SLICES OR CUBES

3 TO 4 CHERRY TOMATOES

1 THIN SLICE RED ONION, SEPARATED INTO RINGS

2 STRIPS BACON, CUT INTO 1-INCH LENGTHS AND SAUTÉED
   OR BROILED UNTIL CRISP

1 TEASPOON OLIVE OIL

FEW DROPS OF LEMON JUICE

SEA SALT

FRESHLY GROUND BLACK PEPPER

1. Layer the ingredients into a salad bowl or lunch container in the following order: romaine, turkey, avocado, tomato, red onion, and bacon.

2. Drizzle the oil evenly over the salad and season with lemon juice, salt, and pepper.

3. Serve immediately or pack in an insulated lunch bag.

Italian Sub Salad

There are a number of simple substitutions in here: a bed of crunchy spinach, dressed with some sesame seeds, adds the flavor and some of the texture you might miss from a traditional deli sub; natural and nitrate-free versions of salami, pepperoni, and beef (found at most delis) replace the standard versions; and a zesty dressing provides richness in place of cheese.

2 CHERRY TOMATOES, QUARTERED

2 TABLESPOONS CHOPPED ROASTED RED PEPPERS

1 TABLESPOON MINCED GREEN OR RED ONIONS

2 BLACK OLIVES, PITTED AND SLICED (OPTIONAL)

1 TEASPOON OLIVE OIL

½ TEASPOON RED WINE VINEGAR

¼ TEASPOON SPICY BROWN MUSTARD

PINCH OF DRIED OREGANO

SEA SALT

FRESHLY GROUND PEPPER

1 TO 1½ CUPS BABY SPINACH

1 TABLESPOON SESAME SEEDS

2 SLICES SALAMI (ABOUT 1 OUNCE)

2 SLICES PEPPERONI (ABOUT 1 OUNCE)

1 SLICE ROAST BEEF (ABOUT 1 OUNCE)

1. In a small bowl, combine the tomatoes, peppers, onions, and olives (if using). Add the olive oil, vinegar, mustard, oregano, salt, and pepper. Toss until evenly coated.

2. Put the baby spinach in a salad bowl. Sprinkle the sesame seeds evenly over the spinach.

3. Make two rolls by layering the following: salami, pepperoni, and roast beef. Use a slotted spoon to lift the tomato mixture from the bowl, letting the

dressing drain back into the bowl, and divide it evenly between the rolls. Roll the meats around the filling and arrange on top of the spinach. Pour the juices from the tomato mixture over the rolls.

4. Serve immediately or pack into an insulated lunch bag.

Taco Bowl

MAKES 4 BOWLS (OR 1 LARGE PLATTER)

Put the filling and the salsa together while you are making dinner the night before, or if you've made tacos for dinner one night, make extra filling to use in this salad. The filling improves in flavor after sitting in the refrigerator for one or two days. Feel free to substitute other ground meats like turkey, buffalo, or venison in this recipe if you prefer.

FOR THE TACO TOPPING

1 TABLESPOON OLIVE OIL

½ CUP MINCED ONIONS

½ CUP MINCED RED OR GREEN BELL PEPPER

1 TABLESPOON CHILI POWDER

1 TEASPOON GROUND CUMIN

½ TEASPOON MILD PAPRIKA

3 TABLESPOONS TOMATO PASTE

1 POUND GRASS-FED GROUND BEEF

FOR THE TACO BOWL

4 CUPS SHREDDED ROMAINE

1 CUP SALSA (PAGE 49)

KALE CHIPS (PAGE 96) OR ZUCCHINI CHIPS (PAGE 97) (OPTIONAL)

To make the taco topping:

1. In a skillet over medium heat, heat the oil. Add the onions, peppers, chili powder, cumin, and paprika. Sauté until the onions are tender, stirring frequently, about 5 minutes. Add the tomato paste and stir into the onions. Continue to sauté until it smells sweet and takes on a brick color, 2 to 3 minutes.

2. Add the ground beef and stir well to break it up. Increase the heat to medium-high and simmer until the beef is fully cooked. Transfer to a bowl and let cool.

To assemble the taco bowl:

1. Divide the romaine evenly among serving bowls or mound on a platter. Add the taco topping and then the salsa. Top with Kale Chips or Zucchini Chips (if using), or pack them separately for lunches.

2. Serve immediately or pack into an insulated lunch bag.

Asian-Style Roast Pork Salad

MAKES 4 SERVINGS

Serve this on its own or tucked into an endive or radicchio cup. The dressing pairs well with a variety of other ingredients. It is a perfect substitute for bottled Asian marinades that typically include soy, an ingredient that is not in the Paleo diet. For a more intense version of this salad, let everyone add a few additions of their own: a pinch of cracked red pepper flakes or a bit of minced chile. Choose peppers and chiles according to your tolerance for heat, from jalapeño to Thai bird to Scotch bonnet.

FOR THE DRESSING

3 TABLESPOONS OLIVE OIL

2 TEASPOONS DARK SESAME OIL

2 TEASPOONS COCONUT AMINOS

2 TEASPOONS TAHINI OR ALMOND BUTTER

½ TEASPOON FINELY GRATED ORANGE ZEST

½ TEASPOON MINCED GINGER

½ TEASPOON MINCED GARLIC

FRESHLY GROUND BLACK PEPPER

FOR THE SALAD

1 POUND SLICED OR SHREDDED ROAST PORK

½ CUP DICED ORANGE SEGMENTS

2 TABLESPOONS MINCED RED ONION

¼ CUP SHREDDED CABBAGE

4 BROCCOLI FLORETS

1 STALK CELERY, THINLY SLICED

1 GREEN ONION, WHITE AND LIGHT-GREEN PORTIONS,
    THINLY SLICED ON AN ANGLE

2 TABLESPOONS MINCED PARSLEY, CHIVES, OR CILANTRO (OPTIONAL)

2 TABLESPOONS SESAME SEEDS (OPTIONAL)

To make the dressing:

In a small bowl, whisk together the olive oil, sesame oil, coconut aminos, tahini, orange zest, ginger, and garlic until evenly blended. Season with pepper. If made in advance, store in the refrigerator in a covered container. It will keep for up to 1 week.

To make the salad:

1. In a bowl, combine the pork, oranges, red onion, cabbage, broccoli, celery, green onion, and sesame seeds (if using). Add the dressing and toss to combine.

2. Transfer to a salad plate or lunch container, or tuck it into an endive or radicchio cup. Scatter with fresh herbs and sesame seeds, if using.

3. Serve immediately or pack into an insulated lunch container.

Sesame "Noodle" Salad with Beef and Broccoli

MAKES 4 SALADS

Use leftover steaks or roasts to make this salad. If you've got some roasted spaghetti squash left over from dinner, this salad only takes a few minutes to put together. If you are preparing the squash according to this recipe, you'll have enough left over for dishes like Chicken "Noodle" Soup (page 53) or "Noodles" and Meatballs (page 82) as a replacement for the zucchini noodles.

FOR THE SPAGHETTI SQUASH NOODLES

1 SMALL SPAGHETTI SQUASH

FOR THE SESAME DRESSING

¼ CUP SESAME OR OLIVE OIL

¼ CUP TAHINI

2 TABLESPOONS COCONUT AMINOS OR WHEAT-FREE TAMARI

1 TABLESPOON LEMON JUICE

½ TEASPOON MINCED GARLIC (OPTIONAL)

SEA SALT

FRESHLY GROUND BLACK PEPPER

12 OUNCES SLICED BEEF, CUT INTO BITE-SIZE PIECES

1 CUP BROCCOLI SPEARS, STEAMED IF DESIRED

2 TEASPOONS SESAME SEEDS, TOASTED

½ CUP RED BELL PEPPER STRIPS

To make the spaghetti squash noodles:

1. Preheat the oven to 375°F. Scrub the spaghetti squash, and set it in a baking dish; add a little water and cover with foil. Bake for 20 minutes. Remove the foil and roast uncovered until it is tender and can be pierced easily with a knife, 15 to 20 minutes.

2. Remove the squash from the oven and let it sit until cool enough to handle. Cut it in half lengthwise and scoop out the seeds. (You can save the seeds to

toast or add to granola and other dishes, if you wish.) Use a fork to loosen and pull the squash flesh out and separate it into strands. You will need about 3 cups for this recipe (¾ cup for each salad).

To make the sesame dressing:

1. In a mixing bowl large enough to hold the noodles, combine the oil, tahini, coconut aminos, lemon juice, garlic (if using), salt, and pepper. Whisk until it has a smooth consistency.

2. Add the spaghetti squash noodles to the dressing and toss to coat evenly. Divide the noodles among four bowls and top with the beef and broccoli. Top with sesame seeds and red pepper strips.

3. Serve immediately or pack into an insulated lunch bag.

"Mu Shu" Vegetables with House Plum Sauce

MAKES 1 SERVING

You'll find plenty of ways to enjoy this plum sauce. Try it with roasted or grilled beef, salmon, or tuna. Use it to stir-fry shrimp or chicken. Swap it out for ketchup with sweet potato fries. You'll always have a use for it.

One way to encourage kids to eat a variety of foods is always to give them control over how it gets from the plate to their tummies. You provide the raw materials but they get to decide how many vegetables, how much meat, and how much sauce goes into each bite.

1½ POUNDS SANTA ROSA OR GREENGAGE PLUMS, PITTED
    AND CUT INTO CHUNKS
¼ CUP WATER
2 LARGE GARLIC CLOVES, PEELED AND ROUGHLY CHOPPED
¾ TEASPOON WHOLE CORIANDER SEED
1 TEASPOON WHOLE FENNEL SEED
⅛ TEASPOON CAYENNE PEPPER
½ TEASPOON SEA SALT
RAW HONEY (OPTIONAL)
2 CRÊPES (PAGE 32), FOLDED INTO QUARTERS
1 CUP SHREDDED VEGETABLES (CELERY, RED ONION,
    BROCCOLI STEMS, CABBAGE, OR KALE), COOKED OR RAW
4 OUNCES COOKED PORK OR CHICKEN, SHREDDED OR FINELY CUT

To make the plum sauce:

1. In a saucepan over medium-high heat, combine the plums and water. Bring to a simmer and cook, stirring frequently, until the plums are very tender, about 20 minutes. Place in a blender and purée.

2. Return the puréed plums to the saucepan and add the garlic, coriander, fennel, cayenne, and salt. Simmer over medium heat until thickened, 15 to 20 minutes. Add raw honey to taste, if using. Let the sauce cool.

3. Arrange the crêpes, vegetables, and pork on a plate or in a lunch container. Fill a small cup with some of the plum sauce to serve on the side. The sauce will keep in a covered container in the refrigerator for up to 3 weeks.

Prosciutto-Wrapped Individual Frittatas

MAKES 4 MUFFINS

Kale is important as much for its looks as its nutrition in these appealing frittatas. If you don't want the added sodium from prosciutto, you can substitute other sliced meats or leave it out altogether.

2 THIN SLICES PROSCIUTTO, CUT INTO QUARTERS

6 EGGS

½ CUP RED ONION

2 TEASPOONS MINCED GARLIC

1 CUP SHREDDED KALE

1 SMALL ZUCCHINI, QUARTERED LENGTHWISE AND
    THEN SLICED CROSSWISE

½ CUP CUBED, COOKED SWEET POTATO OR SQUASH

SEA SALT

FRESHLY GROUND BLACK PEPPER

GARNISHES (PER BOX)

2 OR 3 BELL PEPPER STICKS (RED, YELLOW, OR ORANGE)

3 FENNEL OR CELERY STICKS

3 CUCUMBER SLICES

4 PINEAPPLE CHUNKS

1. Preheat the oven to 350°F. Line eight muffin cups or individual custard cups with prosciutto.

2. In a large bowl, break the eggs and whisk until uniformly yellow.

3. In a cast-iron or an ovenproof nonstick skillet over medium-high heat, heat the oil. Add the onion and garlic and sauté, stirring frequently, until tender but not brown, about 3 minutes. Add the kale and zucchini, and cook until hot and most of the liquid has cooked away, about 2 minutes. Fold in the sweet potatoes, and season with salt and pepper.

4. Divide the kale-and-sweet-potato mixture evenly among the prosciutto-lined cups. Pour the eggs over the vegetables, filling the cups to within a half-inch of the rim. Bake until the eggs are fully cooked and set, about 20 minutes.

5. Remove from the oven and let the frittatas cool in the pan for 5 minutes before removing them.

6. To assemble a bento box, add two frittatas and as many garnishes as you wish.

"Green Egg" Muffins in a Bento Box

MAKES 4 BENTO BOXES (8 MUFFINS)

Use any fresh or cooked leafy greens you like for this recipe. Small diced, colorful vegetables like asparagus or green beans are good too. In fact, this is a good way to use up odds and ends that you may have in the refrigerator. Once you've baked them into these savory muffins, you can keep them for up to two days in the refrigerator. Give them time to return to room temperature (usually not a problem if you are packing them into containers for lunch).

COCONUT OIL OR LARD, FOR GREASING MUFFIN PAN
5 EGGS
1 GREEN ONION, CUT INTO CHUNKS
1 SMALL ZUCCHINI, SLICED
½ CUP ROASTED RED AND YELLOW BELL PEPPER STRIPS
2 CUPS CHOPPED KALE
3 SLICES NITRATE-FREE BACON, COOKED AND CRUMBLED
SEA SALT
FRESHLY GROUND BLACK PEPPER

GARNISHES (PER BOX)
2 OR 3 CHERRY TOMATOES
3 STRAWBERRIES
3 CUCUMBER SLICES
3 FENNEL OR CELERY STICKS
4 MELON CUBES

1. Preheat the oven to 350°F. Generously grease an 8-cup muffin pan with coconut or lard.

2. In a large bowl, break the eggs and whisk until uniformly yellow.

3. In a food processor, combine the onion, zucchini, and roasted pepper strips and pulse until chopped but not completely smooth. Add to the eggs.

4. Chop the kale in the food processor and add to the eggs. (There is no need to clean the food processor in between the onion and kale.)

5. Mix the eggs and vegetables together well and season with salt and pepper. Pour about 1/4 cup of the mixture into the muffin cups. They should be filled to within 1/4 inch of the rim. Scatter the bacon evenly over the muffins.

6. Bake until the eggs are fully cooked, about 25 minutes. Let the muffins cool in the pan for a few minutes before removing them.

7. To assemble the bento box, add two muffins and as many of the suggested garnishes as you wish.

Lemon Chicken Salad Roll

MAKES 4 SALAD ROLLS

Boneless chicken thighs are the perfect cut for this juicy salad roll. To keep them flat while you are baking them, place a round cake pan on top of the chicken, with a few cans of tomatoes on top to add some weight.

4 BONELESS, SKINLESS CHICKEN THIGHS

1 TABLESPOON OLIVE OIL

2 TABLESPOONS LEMON JUICE

SEA SALT

FRESHLY GROUND BLACK PEPPER

1 CUP BABY SPINACH LEAVES

1 HARD-BOILED EGG, CHOPPED

1 TABLESPOON FINELY CHOPPED TOASTED ALMONDS

1. Preheat the oven to 375°F. Preheat a cast-iron skillet in the oven.

2. In a bowl, toss the chicken with the olive oil, lemon juice, salt, and pepper.

3. Take the skillet from the oven and put the chicken in the skillet in an even layer, skin-side (smooth-side) facing down. Return the skillet to the oven and bake the thighs, turning as needed to brown evenly, until the chicken is fully cooked, about 25 minutes. Let the chicken cool to room temperature before assembling the salad roll. (The chicken can be prepared up to 2 days in advance and kept in the refrigerator, but it will be less pliable than freshly baked chicken.)

4. Make the rolls by laying out the chicken pieces on a work surface. Mound the spinach in the center of each thigh. Top with chopped eggs and walnuts, dividing the ingredients evenly among the chicken pieces.

5. Lift the lower edge of the chicken thigh up and over the filling to enclose it completely. Secure with a sandwich pick or vegetable ribbons (if desired).

6. Serve immediately or pack into an insulated lunch container.

Turkey Avocado Spirals

MAKES 2 WRAPS

If your kids like the flavors of tropical fruit, add thin slices of mango or papaya to this recipe. And for grown-ups, or kids who like a touch of heat, add thin slices of jalapeño or serrano chiles.

2 LARGE ROMAINE LETTUCE LEAVES

4 SLICES TURKEY BREAST (GLUTEN-FREE)

4 TO 5 THIN SLICES AVOCADO

FEW DROPS OF LIME JUICE

2 THIN SLICES TOMATO

1 SLICE BACON, HALVED AND COOKED UNTIL CRISP

FRESHLY GROUND BLACK PEPPER

1. Lay the romaine leaves on a clean work surface. Top each with the turkey and avocado. Sprinkle a few drops of lime juice over the avocado to keep it from browning. Add a layer of tomato and top with the bacon.

2. Roll the spirals up starting from the longest edge. Use a serrated knife to cut into 2-inch lengths. The spiral pattern will be visible.

3. Serve immediately or pack into an insulated lunch container.

Waldorf Wrap

A classic Waldorf salad is a perfect Paleo dish, made with fresh apples, celery, raisins, and walnuts, and dressed with a little mayonnaise. It has all the right flavors and textures to appeal to kids. This recipe uses fresh grapes to make it even juicier and sweeter, but feel free to substitute with more traditional raisins. You can substitute pears or even mango for the apples to add fresh flavors and colors to a culinary classic.

FOR THE WALDORF SALAD

1 TART APPLE (SUCH AS GRANNY SMITH), CORED
    AND CHOPPED INTO SMALL PIECES

1 STALK CELERY

1 TABLESPOON CHOPPED WALNUTS OR PECANS

5 OR 6 GRAPES, SLICED

1 TABLESPOON PALEO MAYONNAISE (PAGE 50)

FEW DROPS OF LEMON JUICE (OPTIONAL)

SEA SALT

FRESHLY GROUND BLACK PEPPER

FOR THE WRAPS

2 SLICES TURKEY BREAST (GLUTEN-FREE) OR OTHER SLICED MEAT

To make the salad:

In a small bowl combine the apple, celery, walnuts, grapes, and mayonnaise. Season with a few drops of lemon juice, if using, and salt and pepper.

To assemble the wraps:

1. Lay the turkey slices on a clean work surface. Divide the salad evenly between them, then fold the right and left sides of each turkey slice toward the center. Roll up the wrap, starting at the edge closest to you. Secure with a sandwich pick or vegetable ribbons, if desired.

2. Serve immediately or pack into an insulated lunch container.

Southwest Chicken Wraps

MAKES 2 WRAPS (1 SERVING)

Jicama and sweet red peppers add special flavors and textures to this dish that your kids will really enjoy. Jicama may be new to them, but adding it to carrot slaw tucked inside sliced chicken is a great way to introduce different flavors into their repertoire. Add some sliced avocado or Guacamole (page 112) to round out this wrap and add some healthful fats to lunch.

2 CRÊPES (PAGE 32)

4 TEASPOONS BARBECUE SAUCE (PAGE 121)

¾ CUP COOKED SHREDDED CHICKEN

2 TABLESPOONS SHREDDED JICAMA

2 TABLESPOONS SHREDDED CARROT

1 TABLESPOON MINCED RED BELL PEPPER

6 WHOLE CILANTRO LEAVES (OPTIONAL)

1. Lay the crêpes on a clean work surface. Spread barbecue sauce on each crêpe, then add to each the chicken, jicama, carrot, and pepper. Top with the cilantro leaves, if using.

2. Fold the right and left sides of each crêpe toward the center. Roll the wrap up, starting at the edge closest to you. Secure with a sandwich pick or vegetable ribbons (if desired).

3. Serve immediately or pack into an insulated lunch container.

Curried Tuna Nori Rolls

MAKES 2 WRAPS

Cutting the nori roll into bite-size pieces makes it easier to handle. Use a serrated knife to make a clean cut without tearing the nori.

½ AVOCADO

2 TABLESPOONS OLIVE OIL

1 TABLESPOON LIME JUICE

1 GREEN ONION, THINLY SLICED

2 TEASPOONS SEEDED AND MINCED JALAPEÑO (OPTIONAL)

2 TEASPOONS CURRY POWDER

SEA SALT

FRESHLY GROUND BLACK PEPPER

ONE 5-OUNCE CAN WILD ALBACORE TUNA PACKED IN WATER, DRAINED

2 TEASPOONS BLACK OR GOLDEN RAISINS

1 TEASPOON PINE NUTS OR SLIVERED ALMONDS

FEW DROPS OF LEMON JUICE

2 TOASTED NORI SHEETS

1. In a small bowl, mash the avocado into a chunky paste. Add the oil, lime juice, green onion, jalapeño (if using), and curry powder, and season with salt and pepper.

2. In a mixing bowl, break up the drained tuna into chunks. Add the raisins and pine nuts, and toss until evenly coated. Fold the avocado mixture into the tuna. Add the lemon juice and season with salt and pepper.

3. Lay the nori sheets on a clean work surface so the longer sides are parallel to the edge of your work surface. For each nori, mound the tuna along the long edge of the nori. Lift the upper edge of the nori over the filling to enclose it completely and roll it up the rest of the way.

4. Slice the rolls into pieces, if desired. Serve immediately by arranging on plates, or pack into a lunch container.

Stuffed Grape Leaves

MAKES 20 GRAPE LEAVES (SERVES 4)

If you are a fan of do-ahead cooking, these are perfect for your repertoire. If you are not yet a fan, these might make you a convert. It's hard to argue with plump, delicious grape leaves ready for bento boxes and salads, or on their own for a virtuous and delicious snack.

1 TABLESPOON COCONUT OIL

½ CUP MINCED ONION

1 POUND GRASS-FED GROUND BEEF OR LAMB

1 TEASPOON DRIED OREGANO

½ TEASPOON DRIED PARSLEY

½ TEASPOON GROUND CINNAMON

½ TEASPOON GROUND CUMIN

¼ TEASPOON GROUND NUTMEG

¼ CUP WATER

1 CUP GRATED FRESH CAULIFLOWER

1 TABLESPOON DARK OR GOLDEN SEEDLESS RAISINS

SEA SALT

FRESHLY GROUND BLACK PEPPER

2 DOZEN GRAPE LEAVES, RINSED WELL

1 LEMON, THINLY SLICED

4 BAY LEAVES

1. Preheat the oven to 350°F.

2. In a cast-iron skillet over medium-high heat, heat the oil. Add the onion and sauté, stirring frequently, until tender but not brown, about 3 minutes. Add the beef or lamb and sauté, stirring to break up the meat, until it is cooked through, about 5 minutes. Add the oregano, parsley, cinnamon, cumin, and nutmeg, and sauté until aromatic, about 2 minutes. Add the water, cauliflower, and raisins, and continue to cook until the raisins are plump and hot, 2 to 3 minutes.

continued ▶

3. Lay a grape leaf on a clean work surface with the smooth side facing down. Put 2 to 3 tablespoons of the filling in the center of each leaf, near the stem at the base. Fold the right and left sides of the grape leaf toward the center. Roll the grape leaf up from the bottom. As you finish rolling the grape leaves, arrange them in a single layer in a baking dish.

4. When all of the grape leaves are filled, and the baking dish is packed snug but not too tight, add a few tablespoons of water and top the grape leaves with the lemon slices and bay leaves. Cover the dish with foil and bake until the grape leaves are very hot, about 20 minutes. Remove and discard the sliced lemon and bay leaves.

5. Serve the grape leaves warm, at room temperature, or cold. If made in advance, store in the refrigerator in a covered container. Pour any liquid from the baking dish over the grape leaves to keep them moist. They will keep for up to 5 days.

Turkey Salad–Stuffed Celery Sticks

MAKES 1 SERVING

Send the flavors, colors, and textures of Thanksgiving dinner off to school every day with this salad stuffed into celery boats.

4 OUNCES COOKED TURKEY BREAST, CUBED

½ CUP CUBED COOKED SWEET POTATO

3 TABLESPOONS MINCED RED ONION

2 TEASPOONS DRIED CRANBERRIES

2 TABLESPOONS PALEO MAYONNAISE (PAGE 50)

PINCH OF DRIED THYME

FEW DROPS OF LEMON JUICE

SEA SALT

FRESHLY GROUND BLACK PEPPER

3 OR 4 CELERY STALKS, CUT INTO 5-INCH LENGTHS

1. In a mixing bowl, combine the turkey, sweet potato, onion, and cranberries. Add the mayonnaise and thyme. Toss the salad to combine completely. Add the lemon juice and season with salt and pepper.

2. Divide the salad evenly among the celery stalks.

3. Serve immediately or pack into an insulated lunch container.

Paleo "Noodle" Pizza

MAKES 1 PIZZA

There are pizza crusts based on a variety of nut flours. In this version, the crust is made from thin, crisp zucchini. For the most crunch, eat it straight from the broiler; even though it loses a little crispness in your lunch box, it is always delicious. If you allow a little cheese in your diet, be sure to add some good-quality, grass-fed mozzarella on top.

FOR THE ZUCCHINI CRUST

2 CUPS SHREDDED ZUCCHINI

1 CUP THINLY SLICED ONION

2 TEASPOONS MINCED GARLIC

1 EGG

2 TABLESPOONS OLIVE OIL

FOR THE TOPPING

1 CUP DICED TOMATOES, DRAINED

3 OR 4 THIN SLICES NITRATE-FREE PEPPERONI, CUT INTO STICKS

2 OR 3 LARGE BASIL LEAVES

SEA SALT

FRESHLY GROUND BLACK PEPPER

1. Preheat the broiler to high and adjust an oven rack so that it is about 4 inches from the heat.

2. In a bowl, toss together the zucchini, onion, egg, garlic, and 1 tablespoon of the oil until evenly blended and coated with the egg.

3. In a large skillet over medium-high heat, heat the remaining tablespoon of oil. Add the zucchini mixture to the skillet and spread it in an even layer. Let it cook undisturbed until the bottom layer is golden brown, about 2 minutes. Loosen it from the skillet with a spatula, and invert a plate over the skillet. Flip the crust onto the plate.

4. Return the pan to the heat and slide the crust back into the skillet. Cook the other side until browned and crisp, 2 to 3 minutes.

5. Slide the crust out of the pan and onto a baking sheet. Top with the tomatoes and pepperoni. Tear the basil leaves into pieces and scatter over the top. Salt and pepper to taste. Broil the pizza until the tomatoes are browned and the pepperoni is crisp, about 4 minutes.

6. Serve immediately or pack into an insulated lunch container.

"Noodles" and Meatballs

MAKES 4 SERVINGS

This recipe calls for fresh bulk sausage; in other words, sausage meat without the casings, like ground meat. If you have a reliable source of nitrate-free sausages, this is a simple dish to pull together for lunch at home or in a thermos to take to school. However, making your own is easier than you think. If you find a good sausage that comes in links, slit the casings open and remove the meat. Voilà!

1 POUND FRESH BULK SAUSAGE

1 TABLESPOON OLIVE OIL

1 CUP DICED TOMATOES

2 TEASPOONS MINCED GARLIC

2 CUPS RIBBON-CUT ZUCCHINI

2 CUPS RIBBON-CUT YELLOW SQUASH

½ CUP DICED GREEN OR RED BELL PEPPERS

½ TEASPOON MINCED OREGANO (OPTIONAL)

1. Divide the sausage into 12 equal pieces and shape them into balls. Dip your hands in cold water to keep the meat from sticking.

2. In a sauté pan over medium heat, heat the olive oil. Add the meatballs and cook, turning them to brown evenly, until they are fully cooked, 8 to 9 minutes. Transfer them to a plate using a slotted spoon.

3. Add the tomatoes and garlic to the sauté pan, scraping up any browned bits on the bottom of the pan with a wooden spoon. Bring to a simmer and add the zucchini, yellow squash, and peppers. Sauté over high heat until all of the ingredients are very hot and just tender, about 4 minutes.

4. Use a slotted spoon to transfer the "noodles" to heated plates or vacuum-sealed containers, letting the liquid drain back into the pan.

5. Return the meatballs to the sauté pan and reheat them in the pan juices for about 1 minute. Top the noodles with the meatballs and drizzle any juices in the pan over the top. Scatter with oregano, if using.

6. Serve immediately or pack into an insulated lunch container.

Kebabs

MAKES 2 KEBABS

If you prefer seafood, make these kebabs with shrimp, scallops, or chunks of monkfish. The broiling time will be slightly shorter than for the meat or poultry.

6 CUBES BONELESS BEEF, TURKEY, PORK, OR VEAL (ABOUT 4 OUNCES)

6 MUSHROOM CAPS, STEMS REMOVED

6 LARGE CHUNKS RED OR GREEN BELL PEPPER

6 CHERRY TOMATOES

FOR THE BASTING MIXTURE

2 TABLESPOONS OLIVE OIL

1 TABLESPOON LEMON JUICE

1 TEASPOON MINCED FRESH OREGANO OR ½ TEASPOON DRIED OREGANO

1 TEASPOON MINCED FRESH MINT OR ½ TEASPOON DRIED MINT

2 CUPS COLESLAW (PAGE 56)

1. Preheat the broiler to high and adjust an oven rack so that it is about 3 inches from the heat.

2. Thread the meat, mushrooms, peppers, and tomatoes onto two wooden skewers.

To make the basting mixture:

1. In a small bowl, whisk the oil, lemon juice, oregano, and mint.

2. Place the kebabs on a broiler pan, brush them liberally with the basting mixture, and broil, turning and basting every 2 or 3 minutes, until the meat is cooked through, about 12 minutes.

3. Serve immediately or let the kebabs cool before packing into an insulated lunch container.

Chicken Strips

MAKES 4 SERVINGS

Add a dipping sauce, like Plum Sauce (page 66), Ranch Dressing or Dip (page 111), Barbecue Sauce (page 121), or Salsa (page 49) to this kids' classic done right.

1½ POUNDS BONELESS, SKINLESS CHICKEN PIECES (THIGHS OR BREASTS)
SEA SALT
FRESHLY GROUND BLACK PEPPER
1 EGG
1 TABLESPOON WATER
1 CUP SESAME SEEDS, FOR COATING
3 TABLESPOONS OLIVE OIL, FOR FRYING

1. Cut the chicken pieces into strips the size of an adult's thumb. Season with salt and pepper.

2. In a shallow dish, beat the egg and water together. Pour the sesame seeds into a separate dish.

3. Dip the chicken pieces first into the egg mixture and then into the sesame seeds, pressing the seeds into the surface.

4. In a frying pan over medium-high heat, heat the oil. Add the chicken pieces in a single layer, not touching each other; work in batches if necessary. Fry, turning to brown both sides evenly, until the chicken is fully cooked and the crust is crisp and golden brown, 15 to 16 minutes.

5. Serve immediately, or let the chicken cool and pack into an insulated lunch container.

Turkey Burgers on Sweet Potato Buns

MAKES 4 BURGERS

The tasty buns for this recipe are extra Sweet Potato Pancakes (page 35). That's a good reason to make a double batch next time.

1 POUND GROUND TURKEY

1 EGG

1 TEASPOON MINCED GARLIC OR ½ TEASPOON GARLIC FLAKES

1 TEASPOON CHILI POWDER

SEA SALT

FRESHLY GROUND BLACK PEPPER

1 TABLESPOON OLIVE OIL OR COCONUT OIL

8 SWEET POTATO PANCAKES (PAGE 35)

ADDITIONS AND TOPPINGS (PER BURGER)

2 TO 3 THIN AVOCADO SLICES OR GUACAMOLE

2 TO 3 THIN TOMATO OR RED ONION SLICES

2 TABLESPOONS SALSA (PAGE 49)

1 TABLESPOON RANCH DRESSING OR DIP (PAGE 111)

1. In a medium bowl, combine the turkey, egg, garlic, chili powder, salt, and pepper, and mix together until well incorporated.

2. Divide the turkey mixture into eight equal pieces and shape into patties about 3 inches wide and ½ inch thick.

3. In a sauté pan, heat the oil. Add the patties and cook, turning to brown evenly on both sides, until the turkey is fully cooked, 8 to 9 minutes. Transfer to a plate.

4. Crisp the pancakes in a toaster oven or broiler while preparing the burgers.

5. Make each turkey burger with two pancake buns. Add additional toppings as desired. Serve immediately or pack into an insulated lunch container.

Sausage Sliders on Zucchini Fritters

MAKES 4 SERVINGS

These zucchini fritters are a dish you'll want to serve at many other meals. You can top them with tomatoes, crumbled sausage, and a little cheese (if it's in your diet) to broil for a snack or appetizer; layer them with ground meat and tomato sauce to make a pasta-free lasagna; or make them bigger and wider to use as wraps for sandwiches.

FOR THE ZUCCHINI FRITTERS

1 MEDIUM ZUCCHINI, COARSELY GRATED

2 EGGS

1 TABLESPOON MINCED GREEN ONION

2 TO 3 FRESH BASIL LEAVES, FINELY SHREDDED

1 TEASPOON ALMOND OR COCONUT FLOUR

SEA SALT

FRESHLY GROUND BLACK PEPPER

1 POUND BREAKFAST SAUSAGE (PAGE 37) OR PURCHASED
   NITRATE-FREE FRESH SAUSAGE

2 TO 3 TABLESPOONS OLIVE OR COCONUT OIL

1. In a bowl, combine the zucchini, eggs, green onion, basil, almond flour, salt, and pepper. Stir well to form a batter. Set aside.

2. Divide the sausage into eight equal pieces and shape them into patties about 2 inches wide and 1/4 inch thick. Dip your hands in cold water to keep the meat from sticking.

3. In a sauté pan, heat 1 tablespoon of the oil. Add the patties and cook, turning to brown on both sides evenly, until the sausage is fully cooked, 8 to 9 minutes. Transfer to a plate.

4. Add 1 tablespoon of the oil to the pan, and when the oil is hot, drop the zucchini batter in by the tablespoon, leaving about 3 inches between each fritter. Use 3 tablespoons of batter for each fritter, spreading them out with the back of a spoon into 2-inch-wide fritters. Fry on the first side until browned, about 3 minutes. Turn once and brown on the other side for 2 minutes. Continue making fritters with the remaining batter, adding oil to the pan if needed. You should have 16 thin fritters.

5. Make a sausage patty sandwich with two fritters. Serve immediately or pack into an insulated lunch container.

Peppers Stuffed with Pork and Cabbage

These stuffed peppers are good either served cold or baked as a more traditional stuffed-pepper dish. Keep the filled peppers, fresh or baked, in a covered container in the refrigerator up to a few days so they are easy to pack for lunch. This is one lunch that probably won't get traded.

3 TABLESPOONS OLIVE OIL

1 TABLESPOON LEMON JUICE

½ TEASPOON MINCED GARLIC

SEA SALT

FRESHLY GROUND BLACK PEPPER

1 POUND SLICED OR SHREDDED ROAST PORK

2 TABLESPOONS MINCED RED ONION

¼ CUP SHREDDED RED CABBAGE

1 GREEN ONION, WHITE AND LIGHT-GREEN PORTION,
    THINLY SLICED ON AN ANGLE

2 TABLESPOONS ROASTED RED BELL PEPPER STRIPS

2 TABLESPOONS MINCED PARSLEY OR CILANTRO (OPTIONAL)

2 TEASPOONS PINE NUTS (OPTIONAL)

4 RED OR YELLOW BELL PEPPERS, HALVED AND SEEDED

1. In a mixing bowl, whisk together the olive oil, lemon juice, and garlic until evenly blended. Season with salt and pepper. Add the pork, red onion, cabbage, green onion, roasted pepper strips, parsley (if using), and pine nuts (if using), and toss to combine. The salad can be made in advance to this point and kept in a covered container in the refrigerator for up to 3 days.

2. Fill the peppers with the salad, dividing it evenly among the halves.

3. Serve immediately or pack into an insulated lunch container.

Greek Meatballs, Bento Style

MAKES 4 BENTO BOXES

Flavorful meatballs—made as spicy as you like—served with a cooling yogurt-cucumber dip is a perennial favorite. Make a sample meatball to taste so you are happy with the flavor. For additional heat, you can add some jalapeño with the onions, or sprinkle in some red pepper flakes along with the sea salt and black pepper. Strictly speaking, yogurt is not normally suggested, but if your Paleo diet permits an occasional splurge on Greek yogurt, this is a great recipe for it. Make a double batch of meatballs to have on hand; they freeze well.

FOR THE MEATBALLS

1 POUND GROUND TURKEY

1 LARGE ONION, GRATED

2 EGGS

¼ CUP ALMOND FLOUR

1 TABLESPOON MINCED FENNEL GREENS

1 TABLESPOON MINCED FENNEL BULB

1 TABLESPOON LEMON JUICE

1 TEASPOON GRATED LEMON ZEST

1 TEASPOON MINCED GARLIC

1 TEASPOON GARLIC POWDER

¼ TEASPOON MINCED FRESH MINT OR SLIGHTLY LESS DRIED MINT

¼ TEASPOON DRIED OREGANO

PINCH OF ROSEMARY

½ TEASPOON SEA SALT

¼ TEASPOON FRESHLY GROUND PEPPER

OLIVE OR COCONUT OIL FOR FRYING

FOR THE RAITA SAUCE

1 CUP GREEK YOGURT

1 CUP GRATED CUCUMBER, DRAINED AND SQUEEZED

2 TEASPOONS MINCED GARLIC OR ½ TEASPOON GARLIC POWDER

1 TEASPOON LEMON JUICE

SEA SALT

continued ▶

GARNISHES (PER BOX)

2 ROMAINE SPEARS (TAKEN FROM HEART)

2 CUCUMBER SPEARS

4 OLIVES

3 FENNEL OR CELERY STICKS

2 TOMATO WEDGES

2 HARD-BOILED EGG WEDGES

GRILLED OR ROASTED VEGETABLES, CUT INTO SEVERAL
    STRIPS AND TOSSED TOGETHER

To make the meatballs:

1. Combine the turkey, onion, eggs, almond flour, fennel greens and bulb, lemon juice and zest, garlic, garlic powder, mint, oregano, rosemary, salt, and pepper in a large bowl and mix with a wooden spoon until all of the spices are fully incorporated. Roll into small meatballs.

2. In a pan over medium-high heat, heat a little oil. Make a small meatball and cook until cooked through. Taste it and make seasoning adjustments with herbs, salt, and pepper.

3. In a skillet over medium-high heat, heat enough oil to generously coat bottom of skillet. Add the meatballs in batches, turning them as necessary to cook through and brown on all sides, about 10 minutes.

To make the raita sauce:

Combine the yogurt, cucumber, garlic, lemon juice, and salt. Stir until blended.

To assemble the bento box:

Put two meatballs into a compartment, fill another with the sauce, and fill the remaining compartments with as many of the suggested garnishes as you wish.

Roast Beef Roulades

Roast beef from your kitchen, or even a good deli brand of roast beef, sliced thin, is the perfect wrap to fill with crunchy vegetables. The sauce can be varied; try mustard or Paleo Mayonnaise (page 50) in this roulade. They both add healthful fats to this appealing lunch.

2 THIN SLICES GRASS-FED ROAST BEEF (ABOUT 1½ OUNCES EACH)

2 TEASPOONS ROMESCO DIP (PAGE 110)

5 OR 6 THIN SLICES CUCUMBER

2 TABLESPOONS SHREDDED CARROTS

2 STICKS RED PEPPER

2 SPEARS ASPARAGUS

2 CHERRY TOMATOES, HALVED

1. Lay the beef slices on a clean work surface. Spread the beef with Romesco dip. Layer the filling evenly on each slice, beginning with the cucumbers, then adding the carrots, pepper strips, asparagus, and cherry tomatoes. Roll up the roulade and secure with vegetable ribbons, if desired.

2. Serve immediately or pack into an insulated lunch container.

CHAPTER FIVE KID-FRIENDLY SNACKS

KALE CHIPS

ZUCCHINI CHIPS

PLANTAIN CHIPS

"POPCORN"

MINI-PIZZA BITES

GRANOLA BARS

TRAIL MIX

CREAMY COCONUT FRUIT POPS

SESAME CRACKERS

NUT CHEESE

HUMMUS

ZUCCHINI FRIES

SPINACH ARTICHOKE DIP

ROMESCO DIP

RANCH DRESSING OR DIP

GUACAMOLE

Kid-Friendly Snacks

Your kids get hungry around the clock, so be ready with snacks that are satisfying. Simple is the best strategy for keeping your kids' Paleo plan on track. Some snacks do take a little last-minute assembly and heating (like Pizza Bites), but there are several that can be made ahead and ready to go.

A snack can be anything from a handful of nuts and a piece of fruit to a cup of soup or a few slices of meat. The recipes in this chapter are simple enough to enjoy regularly. Some will find their way into a number of other dishes. Nut cheese is a perfect example of a versatile dish that can be used from breakfast to dessert.

Add Trail Mix or Sesame Crackers to fresh fruit snacks or Plantain Chips to satisfy the urge for something crunchy. A frozen pop made with coconut cream can be just the right amount of creamy to satisfy everyone on a hot summer day.

Remember to use portion-control tricks, like cups that hold just enough dip for one, or bowls that hold a single serving. Even though these recipes are good for you and your kids, it's always smart to be conscious not only of what you are eating, but also how much of it.

Kale Chips

MAKES 5 TO 6 CUPS

Kale has the best overall texture for baking into light, crunchy chips. Putting these chips together is the perfect job for young kitchen helpers, since no knives are needed. If you do end up with leftovers, you can store the chips in an airtight container at room temperature for one or two days. Re-crisp them in a 275°F oven for a few minutes.

COOKING SPRAY

1 HEAD OF KALE, SEPARATED INTO LEAVES, WASHED,
   AND THOROUGHLY DRIED

2 TABLESPOONS OLIVE OIL

SEA SALT, FOR SPRINKLING

FEW DROPS OF LEMON JUICE (OPTIONAL)

1. Preheat the oven to 275°F. Spray two or three baking sheets with cooking oil.

2. In a large bowl, toss the kale leaves with the olive oil to coat evenly. Transfer to baking sheets and bake until the leaves are very crisp, about 20 minutes.

3. Sprinkle the chips with salt and lemon juice, if using, while they are still hot. Serve immediately.

Zucchini Chips

MAKES 4 CUPS (8 SERVINGS)

You can make chips out of a number of different vegetables, including sweet potatoes, beets, yellow squash, and Japanese eggplant, by following this basic recipe. Best of all, there are a variety of seasonings to use.

1 ZUCCHINI (ABOUT 10 OUNCES)
1 TABLESPOON OLIVE OR COCONUT OIL
SEA SALT
FRESHLY GROUND BLACK PEPPER

1. Preheat the oven 450°F. Line two baking sheets with parchment paper.

2. Trim off and discard the zucchini ends and slice them very thin with a mandoline, Benriner, or the slicing attachment of a food processor.

3. In a large bowl, toss the zucchini slices with the oil to coat evenly. Place in a single layer on baking sheets and season with salt and pepper. Bake until the slices are very crisp, about 20 minutes. Serve immediately.

Seasoning Suggestions

Add garlic, seeds, or minced or ground herbs to the zucchini when you toss it with the oil. Or choose one of the following combinations:

- Rosemary and garlic, finished with a few drops of lemon juice
- Chili powder and cumin, finished with a few drops of lime juice
- Oregano and basil
- Few drops coconut aminos or gluten-free tamari
- Few drops lemon or lime juice

Plantain Chips

MAKES 4 CUPS

Serve these whenever you would have reached for tortilla chips. They are great with salsa and guacamole, but they also make a good accompaniment to stews and salads.

2 PLANTAINS (ABOUT 10 OUNCES)
OLIVE OR COCONUT OIL FOR FRYING
SEA SALT
FRESHLY GROUND BLACK PEPPER
LIME JUICE (OPTIONAL)

1. Slice the plantains lengthwise into long thin strips or crosswise for thin rounds, about ¼ inch thick.

2. Add enough oil to fill a deep skillet to a depth of ¼ inch. Heat the oil over medium heat until it reaches about 350°F. When it is ready the oil should shimmer and form bubbles when a plantain slice is dipped into it.

3. Fry the plantain slices in batches; they should not overlap as they fry. Turn them to brown evenly on both sides until golden and crisp, about 5 minutes. Drain the chips on a cooling rack or on a plate lined with paper towel. Season with salt, pepper, and lime juice, if using. Serve immediately.

"Popcorn"

MAKES 4 CUPS (8 SERVINGS)

You can use any of the flavoring suggestions for Zucchini Chips (page 97) to add some extra flavor to this snack. Be sure you roast the cauliflower long enough to give it a toasty, nutty aroma and taste.

1 HEAD CAULIFLOWER
4 TABLESPOONS OLIVE OIL
1 TEASPOON SALT

1. Preheat the oven 425°F. Line two baking sheets with parchment paper or brush with olive or coconut oil.

2. Remove the core of the cauliflower with a paring knife and break the head apart into small florets that are about the same size as popcorn.

3. In a large bowl, toss the cauliflower with the olive oil to coat evenly. Place in a single layer on baking sheets, and season with salt and pepper. Bake until the "popcorn" is very crisp, about 20 minutes. Serve immediately.

Mini-Pizza Bites

MAKES 20 BITES

Crisping the pepperoni makes all the difference. When you spread the tomato sauce on the pizza bites, don't overdo it. There should be just enough to coat so that it cooks into a tangy glaze.

20 SLICES OF PEPPERONI
3 TABLESPOONS TOMATO SAUCE (PAGE 124)
1 TEASPOON SHREDDED OREGANO LEAVES
1 TEASPOON SHREDDED BASIL LEAVES

1. Preheat the oven 400°F. Line a baking sheet with parchment paper or a wire rack.

2. Place the pepperoni slices in a single layer on the baking sheet. Bake until crisp, about 5 minutes. Turn the slices once to crisp each side evenly.

3. Remove the baking sheet from the oven and spread each pepperoni slice with a little tomato sauce and a pinch of oregano and basil. Add other toppings as desired (see suggestions below) and return to the oven. Bake for another 4 to 5 minutes. Serve immediately.

Topping Suggestions:

There are many additional toppings that can be used. Be sure to cut them small enough to fit onto the pepperoni:

- Grated mozzarella or an aged cheese like Asiago
- Slivered black olives
- Matchsticks of multicolored bell peppers
- Thin mushroom slices
- Green onions, thinly sliced on the diagonal

Granola Bars

MAKES 18 BARS

Granola bars do not have to be candy bars in disguise. These bars, for instance, combine nuts, seeds, dried fruit, and unsweetened coconut. Treat this recipe as a blueprint to create your own family favorites by combining two or more types of nuts or seeds, or use your own special blend of dried fruit. The honey is used sparingly, but you do need it to help hold the granola bars together. Break a granola bar up into chunks, add some nut or coconut milk, and you've got an instant breakfast or snack.

1½ CUPS SLICED ALMONDS

1½ CUPS FINELY SHREDDED UNSWEETENED COCONUT

¾ CUP MINI CHOCOLATE CHIPS (OPTIONAL)

½ CUP CHOPPED UNSWEETENED DRIED FRUIT (OPTIONAL)

½ CUP BLANCHED ALMOND OR COCONUT FLOUR

⅓ CUP HULLED SUNFLOWER SEEDS

⅓ CUP COCONUT OIL, MELTED

¼ CUP ALMOND BUTTER

¼ CUP RAW HONEY

1 TABLESPOON SESAME SEEDS

1 TEASPOON VANILLA EXTRACT

¾ TEASPOON BAKING SODA

1. Preheat the oven to 325°F. Line a 9-by-13-inch baking pan with a piece of parchment paper long enough to extend over the rim of the pan by 2 inches on each side.

2. In a large bowl, combine the almonds, coconut, chocolate chips (if using), dried fruit (if using), almond flour, sunflower seeds, coconut oil, almond butter, honey, sesame seeds, vanilla, and baking soda, and stir until well incorporated. Transfer the mixture to the prepared baking pan and press it

continued ▶

into an even layer. Bake until puffed and golden on the edges and top, about 20 minutes. As soon as the pan comes out of the oven, press the granola flat with a spatula.

3. Cool completely and then refrigerate for at least 2 hours.

4. Lift the granola out of the pan using the parchment paper. Cut into bars or squares. Wrap individually and store in the refrigerator for up to 2 weeks.

Trail Mix

MAKES 2 CUPS

Choose the nuts, seeds, and dried fruits you like for a custom version of trail mix that travels well, for instant gratification in a healthful, balanced, and delicious snack.

1 CUP RAW PUMPKIN SEEDS

½ CUP SLIVERED ALMONDS

⅓ CUP WALNUTS

⅓ CUP PECANS

½ CUP UNSWEETENED LARGE COCONUT FLAKES, TOASTED

⅓ CUP CHOPPED PITTED DATES

¼ CUP CHOPPED DRIED MANGO OR PEACH

½ TEASPOON SEA SALT

1. Preheat the oven 350°F. Line two baking sheets with parchment paper.

2. On one of the baking sheets, combine the pumpkin seeds, almonds, walnuts, and pecans and spread in an even layer. Spread the coconut flakes on the other baking sheet.

3. Bake until the pumpkin seeds and nuts are toasted and golden, 12 to 13 minutes, and the coconut flakes are golden-brown on the edges and slightly crisp, 10 to 12 minutes. When done, transfer to a bowl. Add the dates, mango or peach, and sea salt. Toss to distribute evenly.

4. Store trail mix in an airtight container at room temperature for up to 3 weeks.

Creamy Coconut Fruit Pops

You can find freezer-pop molds at most houseware shops, from simple to high-tech. The Cadillac of all freezer pop makers is Zoku's Quick Pop Maker, capable of making fully frozen pops in about 7 minutes.

ONE 14-OUNCE CAN COCONUT MILK (FULL-FAT)
2 TABLESPOONS RAW HONEY OR GRADE B MAPLE SYRUP
1½ CUPS BERRIES OR CHOPPED FRUIT, FRESH OR FROZEN

1. In a bowl, combine the coconut milk and honey.

2. Fill the bottom third of each mold with fruit. Pour or ladle the coconut milk over the fruit. Insert a stick in the center of the mold and freeze until solid, 2 to 3 hours. These pops will keep in the freezer for up to 8 weeks.

Sesame Crackers

If you enjoy the crisp contrast of crackers with soups and stews, this is the perfect choice. It can even bridge the "grilled cheese" gap when you've got a great pot of tomato soup on the stove.

1 CUP SUNFLOWER SEEDS

1 CUP SESAME SEEDS

5 TABLESPOONS WATER

SEA SALT

FRESHLY GROUND BLACK PEPPER

1. Preheat the oven 350°F. Line a baking sheet with parchment paper and cut a second piece of the same length to roll out the dough on later.

2. In a food processor, grind the sunflower and sesame seeds to a coarse meal; pulse the machine off and on to avoid making a butter. Add the water to the seeds and process until you have a heavy dough that rides on the top of the blade.

3. Transfer the dough to the lined baking sheet and top with the second sheet. Use a rolling pin to roll the cracker dough out into an even layer. Remove the top sheet of parchment paper and score the dough into individual crackers with a sharp knife or a pizza cutter. Sprinkle with salt and pepper.

4. Bake until the edges and bottom are golden, 20 minutes. Let the crackers cool in the pan and then lift them out of the pan with a palette knife, breaking them into crackers along the lines you scored.

5. Store crackers in an airtight container at room temperature for up to 2 weeks.

Nut Cheese

Draining the nut cheese gives it a good, spreadable consistency so it can stand in for cream cheese quite well. The texture is somewhat similar to ricotta cheese, which it can also stand in for as a topping or filling. Finally, you can stir it into soups for a creamy finish and body without adding dairy.

3 CUPS BLANCHED WHOLE ALMONDS, HAZELNUTS, CASHEWS,
   OR MACADAMIA NUTS
1½ CUPS FILTERED WATER
2 TEASPOONS UNFILTERED APPLE CIDER VINEGAR
2 TEASPOONS LEMON JUICE
1 TEASPOON SEA SALT

1. In a covered bowl or jar, soak the nuts in the water for 24 hours.

2. Transfer the nuts and the soaking liquid to a food processor and grind to a very smooth paste. Spoon the paste into a cheesecloth- or coffee filter–lined colander set over a bowl to collect the liquid as the cheese drains. Drain for at least 4 hours, or until the nut cheese is thick and spreadable.

3. Stir in the vinegar, lemon juice, and salt. Store in a covered container in the refrigerator for up to 2 weeks.

Hummus

MAKES 3 CUPS

Cauliflower provides body for this hummus, and its mild flavor never gets in the way of the tahini, lemon juice, and garlic that make hummus one of the world's favorite dips.

1 HEAD CAULIFLOWER

2 TABLESPOONS OLIVE OIL

2 TEASPOONS GROUND CUMIN

½ CUP TAHINI

3 CLOVES GARLIC, SMASHED AND MINCED INTO A PASTE

JUICE OF 1 LEMON

SEA SALT

FRESHLY GROUND BLACK PEPPER

1. Preheat the oven 425°F. Line two baking sheets with parchment paper or brush with olive or coconut oil.

2. Using a paring knife, remove the core of the cauliflower and break the head apart into small florets, about 1½ inches long.

3. In a large bowl, toss the cauliflower with the olive oil and cumin to coat evenly. Transfer to baking sheets in a single layer. Bake until tender and golden on the edges, about 25 minutes. Let cool to room temperature.

4. In a food processor, combine the cauliflower, tahini, garlic, lemon juice, salt, and pepper, and process to make a smooth, light paste. If the hummus seems too thick, add a little water.

5. The hummus is ready to serve. Store in a covered container in the refrigerator for up to 5 days; check the consistency and seasoning before serving.

Zucchini Fries

Tomato sauce is a classic accompaniment to this crisp snack food, but also try it with Guacamole (page 112), Romesco Dip (page 110), or Ranch Dressing (page 111).

1 EGG

¼ CUP ALMOND MILK

¾ CUP ALMOND FLOUR

¼ CUP SHREDDED PARMESAN CHEESE (OPTIONAL)

2 TEASPOONS DRIED OREGANO OR ITALIAN SEASONING BLEND

PINCH OF RED PEPPER FLAKES (OPTIONAL)

OLIVE OIL AS NEEDED FOR FRYING

2 ZUCCHINI, CUT INTO STICKS

2 CUPS TOMATO SAUCE (PAGE 124) FOR DIPPING

1. In a bowl, combine the egg and almond milk, and whisk together until smooth.

2. In a separate bowl, combine the almond flour, Parmesan (if using), oregano, and pepper flakes (if using).

3. Add enough oil to fill a deep skillet to a depth of ¼ inch. Heat the oil over medium heat until it reaches 350°F. When it is ready the oil should shimmer, and it will bubble when the edge of a zucchini slice is dipped in.

4. Dip the zucchini pieces first into the egg mixture, then the flour mixture. Add to the hot oil in a single layer and fry, turning to brown them evenly on both sides, until golden and crisp, about 5 minutes. Drain the fries on a cooling rack or on a paper towel–lined plate. Serve immediately with tomato sauce.

Spinach Artichoke Dip

MAKES 4 SERVINGS

Plantain Chips (page 98) or Sesame Crackers (page 105) make the perfect accompaniment to this revised classic.

1 TABLESPOON EXTRA-VIRGIN OLIVE OIL PLUS EXTRA FOR
    COATING BAKING DISH
1 SMALL ONION, DICED (ABOUT 1 CUP)
2 GARLIC CLOVES, MINCED
2 CUPS CHOPPED COOKED OR THAWED FROZEN SPINACH,
    SQUEEZED TO REMOVE MOISTURE
ONE 14-OUNCE CAN BRINE-PACKED ARTICHOKE HEARTS,
    DRAINED AND QUARTERED
2 CUPS NUT CHEESE (PAGE 106)
1 TABLESPOON LEMON JUICE
½ TEASPOON GARLIC POWDER
SEA SALT
FRESHLY GROUND BLACK PEPPER

1. Preheat the oven 400°F. Lightly coat an oval or round baking dish with olive oil.

2. In a saucepan over medium-high heat, heat the oil. Add the onion and sauté until tender and golden brown, about 3 minutes. Add the garlic and sauté until aromatic, 30 seconds. Add the spinach and sauté, stirring frequently, until hot, about 3 minutes.

3. Transfer the spinach to the prepared baking dish and add the artichoke hearts, nut cheese, lemon juice, and garlic powder. Season with salt and pepper.

4. Bake the dip until it is hot and the top is lightly browned, about 15 minutes. Serve immediately.

Romesco Dip

This sweet, smoky sauce is a great accompaniment for everything from roasted sweet potatoes to grilled salmon. Use hazelnuts or walnuts to make your own version if you prefer.

COOKING SPRAY (OPTIONAL)
1 RED BELL PEPPER, HALVED AND SEEDED
3 PLUM TOMATOES, HALVED
¼ CUP BLANCHED WHOLE ALMONDS
1 TO 2 DRIED RED CHILES, BROKEN INTO PIECES
2 GARLIC CLOVES, PEELED
2 TABLESPOONS CHOPPED FRESH OREGANO
2 TABLESPOONS UNFILTERED APPLE CIDER VINEGAR
¼ CUP OLIVE OIL
SEA SALT

1. Preheat the oven to 400°F. Line a baking sheet with parchment paper or spray lightly with cooking spray. Place the pepper, tomatoes, almonds, chiles, and garlic on the baking sheet, and roast until the skin on the pepper is blistered and the almonds are golden-brown, about 15 minutes.

2. Let the vegetables cool for 10 minutes before transferring to a food processor or blender. Add the oregano and vinegar and purée to a coarse but fairly smooth paste. While the machine is running, add the oil in a thin stream. Season with salt.

3. This sauce can be used immediately or stored in a covered container or jar in the refrigerator for up to 2 weeks.

Ranch Dressing or Dip

MAKES 1 CUP (4 SERVINGS)

This is the game changer for many kids when it comes to exploring a new food. You can offer it with nearly everything except dessert, from vegetables to meats to fish to poultry. To make a dip with more body, use Nut Cheese (page 106) instead of nut milk.

½ CUP PALEO MAYONNAISE (PAGE 50)

1 TABLESPOON LEMON JUICE

½ CUP ALMOND OR COCONUT MILK OR ½ CUP NUT CHEESE (PAGE 106)

1 TABLESPOON DRIED DILL

1 TEASPOON GARLIC POWDER

SEA SALT

FRESHLY GROUND BLACK PEPPER

In a bowl, combine the mayonnaise, lemon juice, almond milk, dill, and garlic powder, and season with salt and pepper. This sauce can be stored in a covered container or jar in the refrigerator, and will last for up to 5 days.

Guacamole

Let everyone make their own guacamole right in the avocado shell. Bring out a platter of halved avocados, the garnishes, and the seasonings in little cups, and pass out forks for mashing and eating.

2 CUPS DICED RIPE AVOCADO (ABOUT 2 AVOCADOS)
JUICE OF 1 LIME
2 TEASPOONS MINCED JALAPEÑO (OPTIONAL)
⅓ CUP MINCED RED ONION
⅓ CUP MINCED TOMATO, SEEDED AND DICED
1 TABLESPOON CHOPPED FRESH CILANTRO
SEA SALT
FRESHLY GROUND BLACK PEPPER

In a bowl or mortar and pestle, combine the avocado, lime juice, jalapeño (if using), onion, tomato, cilantro, salt, and pepper, and mash or pound together to a paste as coarse or fine as you wish. Serve immediately.

CHAPTER SIX KID-FRIENDLY DINNERS

Kid-Friendly Dinners

Family dinners are a good time to form your children's healthy habits for eating fresh, healthful foods, as well as cooking to get the most out of them. Keep the seasons in mind when you choose flavors, and let seasonal fruits and vegetables of all sorts round out the meal, providing plenty of colors, textures, and flavors.

Many of the recipes in this chapter can be doubled so you have enough on hand for lunches later in the week. Likewise, you can take a look at the lunch recipes in Chapter Four for some enticing dinner options.

Chicken Piccata

MAKES 4 SERVINGS

Double this recipe to have cooked chicken on hand for lunches for the next few days. A traditional piccata calls for a spoonful of capers in the sauce. If you are not watching sodium, they add a tart, pickled taste and a bit of crunch. This recipes works equally well with veal or pork cutlets and boneless fish fillets.

4 BONELESS, SKINLESS CHICKEN BREAST HALVES (1½ POUNDS)
SEA SALT
FRESHLY GROUND BLACK PEPPER
2 TABLESPOONS OLIVE OIL
¼ CUP BONE BROTH (PAGE 52) OR PREPARED CHICKEN BROTH
¼ CUP LEMON JUICE
¼ CUP FRESH CHOPPED PARSLEY
2 TABLESPOONS BUTTER

1. Pound the chicken breasts lightly with a meat mallet to even the thickness. Season with salt and pepper.

2. In a cast-iron skillet or sauté pan over medium-high heat, heat the oil. Add the chicken breast, smooth-side down, and cook until golden on the first side, about 5 minutes. Lower the heat to medium, turn the chicken, cover the skillet, and continue to cook without disturbing until the chicken is nearly cooked through, another 5 minutes. Do this in batches or in two skillets so the chicken is not crowded in the pan.

3. Remove the cover and transfer the chicken to a heated platter or plates. Increase the heat to high and add the broth to the skillet, stirring to dissolve any burned bits in the pan. When the broth has nearly cooked away, add the lemon juice and the parsley. Add the butter and swirl it into the sauce. Season with salt and pepper. Pour the sauce over the chicken and serve immediately.

Chimichurri Sauce

MAKES 1 CUP

Chimichurri sauce is the classic Argentinian sauce for grilled steaks. Make the sauce as mild or spicy as your kids prefer; fans of spicy foods can always sprinkle red pepper flakes on top. Flat-leaf parsley is best for this dish; its fresh, robust flavor stands up to the garlic and vinegar. Make a big batch of this sauce to keep on hand as an accompaniment to a variety of grilled or roasted meats, poultry, and seafood.

1 CUP COARSELY CHOPPED, FRESH FLAT-LEAF PARSLEY

2 TABLESPOONS FRESH OREGANO LEAVES

3 GARLIC CLOVES, FINELY MINCED

½ CUP OLIVE OIL

2 TABLESPOONS UNFILTERED APPLE CIDER VINEGAR

SEA SALT

FRESHLY GROUND BLACK PEPPER

RED PEPPER FLAKES (OPTIONAL)

In a small bowl, combine the parsley, oregano, garlic, oil, vinegar, salt, pepper, and red pepper flakes (if using). Let rest at room temperature for 20 minutes before serving. This sauce can be prepared in advance and stored in a covered container in the refrigerator for up to 2 days.

Grilled London Broil with Chimichurri Sauce

MAKES 6 SERVINGS

Use thin slices of leftover London broil as a wrapper for any fillings you have on hand, such as vegetable strips, leafy greens, or grilled vegetables.

1 FLANK STEAK (ABOUT 3 POUNDS)
2 TABLESPOONS WALNUT OR OLIVE OIL
1 TABLESPOON UNFILTERED APPLE CIDER VINEGAR
1 GARLIC CLOVE, CHOPPED
2 TEASPOONS CHOPPED FRESH OREGANO
SEA SALT
FRESHLY GROUND BLACK PEPPER
¾ CUP CHIMICHURRI SAUCE (PAGE 117)

1. Put the flank steak in a shallow baking dish. In a small bowl combine the oil, vinegar, garlic, oregano, salt, and pepper and pour over the steak, turning it to coat evenly. Cover and marinate in the refrigerator for at least 1 hour and up to 12 hours.

2. Preheat a grill to medium-high heat (the coals should glow red with a covering of ash). Lift the flank steak from the marinade, letting the oil drain back into the bowl. Grill the steak, turning to brown evenly on both sides, until the steak is rare (135°F) or the doneness you prefer. Transfer to a cutting board and let the steak rest for 10 minutes before slicing.

3. To slice flank steak, make cuts at an angle across the grain. Serve immediately with the chimichurri sauce.

Shepherd's Pie

MAKES 4 SERVINGS

Traditionally made with lamb, this dish is equally good when made with turkey or beef. Make extra filling and topping for assembling individual shepherd's pies that you can refrigerate or freeze for another day's lunch.

FOR THE FILLING

2 TABLESPOONS OLIVE OIL, PLUS MORE FOR GREASING
    THE CASSEROLE DISH

2 STRIPS NITRATE-FREE BACON, CUT INTO 1-INCH PIECES

1 LARGE ONION, DICED

1 POUND GRASS-FED GROUND LAMB

2 CUPS DICED CARROTS

2 CUPS DICED CELERY

1 CUP CHICKEN BROTH

½ TEASPOON DRIED THYME

½ TEASPOON SMOKED PAPRIKA (OPTIONAL)

SEA SALT

FRESHLY GROUND BLACK PEPPER

FOR THE TOPPING

1 LARGE CAULIFLOWER, CORED AND BROKEN INTO FLORETS

2 TABLESPOONS OLIVE OIL

Preheat the oven to 350°F. Brush a casserole or baking dish with olive oil.

To make the filling:

1. In a cast-iron skillet or sauté pan, heat the oil over medium-high heat. Add the bacon and cook until it is crisp, turning as it cooks, for about 2 minutes. Add the onion and sauté, stirring frequently, until tender and just starting to turn golden, 3 minutes.

continued ▶

2. Add the lamb and cook, stirring to break up the meat, until it no longer looks raw, 3 to 4 minutes. Add the carrots, celery, broth, thyme, paprika (if using), salt, and pepper. Stir to combine. Reduce the heat to low, cover, and simmer until the carrots are tender and the filling is flavorful, about 20 minutes. Transfer the filling to the casserole or baking dish.

To make the topping:

1. Steam the cauliflower until it is very tender. Drain in a colander for a few minutes and let the cauliflower cool for at least 10 minutes before transferring to a food processor. Purée the cauliflower until it is very smooth. With the machine running, add the olive oil in a thin stream. When all of the oil has been added, season the purée with salt and pepper. Spoon the cauliflower topping evenly over the surface of the meat in a smooth layer.

2. Bake the shepherd's pie until the topping is golden brown and the filling is very hot, 25 to 30 minutes. Serve immediately.

Barbecue Sauce

MAKES 1½ CUPS

This barbecue sauce does call for a bit of honey—which turns it into a tangy glaze for cooking foods—but it's a far cry from the amount of refined sugar in bottled barbecue sauce. If you have this sauce on hand, you'll have a ready-to-use dipping sauce for cauliflower "Popcorn." Also spread it on chicken, pork, or fish before you bake or grill them, or try it as a topping for burgers.

ONE 6-OUNCE CAN TOMATO PASTE
½ CUP WATER, OR MORE IF NEEDED
3 TABLESPOONS RAW HONEY OR GRADE B MAPLE SYRUP
JUICE OF 1 ORANGE
1 TEASPOON CHILI POWDER, PLUS MORE TO TASTE
1 TEASPOON DRIED ROSEMARY LEAVES, CRUSHED
½ TEASPOON CORIANDER SEEDS, FINELY GROUND OR CRUSHED
1 TEASPOON GROUND GINGER
½ TEASPOON GARLIC POWDER

In a saucepan, combine all the ingredients and bring to a simmer over medium heat. Once the sauce is simmering, it can be used immediately. The sauce can be made in advance and stored in a covered container in the refrigerator for up to 2 weeks. Warm the sauce before using or serving.

Pulled Pork

MAKES 6 TO 8 SERVINGS

This pork has to cook low and slow for several hours, but it is not at all demand-ing. You just have to check it every hour or so while you do something else. Cook the pork in your slow cooker, if you have one, for 12 hours and you'll be rewarded with juicy pork that didn't take any of your attention while it cooked. Serve it on Sweet Potato Pancakes (page 35) for a Paleo sandwich, paired with a side of Coleslaw (page 56).

1 PORK SHOULDER ROAST (4 TO 5 POUNDS)
1 CUP WATER
2 TABLESPOONS DRIED BASIL
2 TEASPOONS DRIED ROSEMARY
SALT
BARBECUE SAUCE (PAGE 121)

1. Preheat the oven to 300°F. Put the pork, fatty-side facing up, in a Dutch oven or similar ovenproof casserole that can hold the pork without crowding.

2. Add the water to the bottom of the Dutch oven; scatter the herbs over the roast and season with salt. Cover tightly with a lid or aluminum foil. Roast until the pork is tender enough to pull apart with a fork, 3½ to 4 hours. Add a little more water to the pot if the drippings are beginning to scorch.

3. Let the roast cool until it can be handled, then pull the meat away from the bones and fat. Shred the meat, combine it with the barbecue sauce, and bring to a simmer over medium heat. Serve immediately.

Lamb Chops with Herbed Mash

MAKES 8 SERVINGS

Lamb chops are a perfect excuse for eating with your fingers at the dinner table, and root vegetable mash is a true comfort food. Try it with other dishes, for instance as a bed for Beef Stew (page 127) or along with Meatloaf (page 130).

FOR THE HERBED MASH

2 PARSNIPS, PEELED AND CUBED

1 CARROT, PEELED AND CUBED

1 PURPLE TURNIP, PEELED AND CUBED

2 TEASPOONS BASIL LEAVES

2 TEASPOONS MARJORAM LEAVES

2 TEASPOONS THYME LEAVES

1 TABLESPOON LEMON JUICE

2 TABLESPOONS OLIVE OIL, PLUS MORE FOR BRUSHING THE LAMB CHOPS

8 GRASS-FED LAMB CHOPS

SEA SALT

FRESHLY GROUND BLACK PEPPER

1. Preheat a broiler to medium-high. Adjust the oven rack to within 6 inches of the broiler.

2. Steam the parsnips, carrot, and turnip until they are very tender. Drain in a colander and then transfer to a mixing bowl. Use a potato masher to make a coarse purée. Add the basil, marjoram, thyme, and lemon juice, and blend. Beat in the olive oil until the mash is smooth. Season with salt and pepper. Keep warm.

3. Brush the lamb chops with olive oil and season with salt and pepper. Transfer to a broiler pan and broil the lamb chops, turning once to cook evenly, to the desired doneness, about 9 minutes for rare (135°F).

4. Serve lamb chops on a bed of mash.

Tomato Sauce

MAKES 6 CUPS

You can find Paleo-friendly tomato sauces with no difficulty, but this sauce is simple to make and only calls for a few simple ingredients that are easy to keep on hand in the pantry.

3 TABLESPOONS OLIVE OIL

4 GARLIC CLOVES, MINCED

8 CUPS SEEDED CHOPPED TOMATOES, FRESH OR CANNED

ONE 6-OUNCE CAN TOMATO PASTE

1 SPRIG OREGANO OR BASIL

SALT

FRESHLY GROUND BLACK PEPPER

1. In a saucepan over medium-high heat, heat the oil. Add the garlic and cook until aromatic, about 30 seconds.

2. Add the tomatoes and tomato paste and stir to combine. Reduce the heat to low and simmer for 15 minutes. Add the oregano and continue to simmer until the sauce is thick and flavorful. Season with salt and pepper.

3. Remove and discard the oregano sprig. Strain the sauce through a sieve for a smooth texture or leave it chunky, if you prefer. Cool the sauce and store it in jars or covered containers in the refrigerator for up to 7 days, or in the freezer for up to 3 months.

Lasagna

Some Paleo plans suggest that you use limited amounts of cheeses like ricotta and mozzarella. The main requirement of a good lasagna seems to be layers of fillings, at least one of which should be creamy and gooey. This lasagna layers vegetables and cheese between chunks of broiled eggplant. Nut cheese provides a creamy, gooey consistency and mimics the texture of traditional ricotta. It's your choice whether or not to add a topping of mozzarella.

1 TABLESPOON OLIVE OIL

4 MINCED GARLIC CLOVES

1 CHOPPED YELLOW ONION

2½ CUPS FROZEN SPINACH (FRESH IF YOU HAVE IT)

1 POUND BREAKFAST SAUSAGE (PAGE 37)

4 CUPS TOMATO SAUCE (PAGE 124)

12 SLICES EGGPLANT, BROILED UNTIL TENDER

1½ CUPS NUT CHEESE (PAGE 106)

2 TEASPOONS MINCED OREGANO

2 TEASPOONS MINCED BASIL

SEA SALT

FRESHLY GROUND BLACK PEPPER

SHREDDED MOZZARELLA FOR TOPPING (OPTIONAL)

1. In a skillet over medium-high heat, heat the oil. Add the garlic and cook until aromatic, about 30 seconds. Add the onion and cook, stirring frequently, until golden, about 4 minutes. Add the spinach and sauté until hot and flavorful, about 2 minutes. Transfer to a bowl and let the spinach cool.

2. Return the skillet to the heat and add the oil. Add the sausage meat and cook, stirring to break it up, until cooked through and browned. Add 1½ cups of the tomato sauce and simmer for 5 minutes.

continued ▶

Lasagna *continued* ▶

To assemble the lasagna:

1. Spoon some of the remaining 2½ cups of tomato sauce into a baking dish. Add half the broiled eggplant in a layer and top the eggplant with half of the nut cheese. Sprinkle with half of the oregano and basil. Next add half the sausage mixture, followed by half the spinach. Repeat layering with remaining ingredients. Pour the remaining tomato sauce evenly over the lasagna and top with the shredded mozzarella, if using.

2. Bake the lasagna until the top is golden and the lasagna is very hot, about 25 minutes. Let the lasagna rest for 10 minutes before cutting into pieces and serving.

Beef Stew

MAKES 6 SERVINGS

The porcini mushrooms are optional in this stew, but they add an earthiness that is impossible to achieve any other way. Their meaty texture goes perfectly with beef. Why not give kids an opportunity to make friends with a food that most won't encounter until they're adults? Serve this with herbed root mash (page 123) or the cauliflower purée in Shepherd's Pie (page 119).

2 TABLESPOONS OLIVE OIL

1 GRASS-FED BEEF EYE ROUND, CUT INTO 2-INCH CUBES

1 ONION, CHOPPED

1 GARLIC CLOVE, DICED

2 TABLESPOONS TOMATO PASTE

½ OUNCE DRIED PORCINI MUSHROOMS (OPTIONAL)

3 CUPS BONE BROTH (PAGE 52), PLUS MORE IF NEEDED

2 THYME SPRIGS OR 1 TEASPOON DRIED THYME LEAVES

1 ROSEMARY SPRIG OR 1 TEASPOON DRIED ROSEMARY

2 CARROTS, SLICED

2 CELERY STALKS, SLICED

1 MEDIUM SWEET POTATO, PEELED AND CUBED

SEA SALT

FRESHLY GROUND BLACK PEPPER

1. In a Dutch oven or flameproof casserole over medium heat, heat the oil. Add the beef in batches and cook, turning, until browned on all sides. Transfer to a plate when all the beef is browned; set aside. Add the onion and garlic, and sauté, stirring frequently, until golden, about 3 minutes. Add the tomato paste and stir into the onions for 1 minute.

2. Add the porcini (if using), the broth, thyme, rosemary, carrots, celery, and sweet potato. Increase the heat until the broth comes to a boil, then lower to a simmer and return the beef to the pot along with any juices.

3. Cover the pot and reduce the heat to low. Simmer until the meat is tender, 1 to 1½ hours. Remove and discard the herb sprigs.

4. The stew can be served immediately, or cooled and stored in a covered container in the refrigerator for up to 4 days, or in the freezer for up to 3 months.

Chicken Fajitas

MAKES 5 SERVINGS

You can substitute other meats for the chicken in this recipe, and if you have some Crêpes (page 32) ready in the refrigerator or freezer, use them instead of the lettuce wraps.

FOR THE FAJITA MARINADE
JUICE OF 1 LEMON
JUICE OF 1 LIME
2 TABLESPOONS OLIVE OR COCONUT OIL
3 GARLIC CLOVES, MINCED
1 TEASPOON GROUND CUMIN
1 TEASPOON DRIED MEXICAN OREGANO
1 TEASPOON CHILI POWDER
1 TEASPOON SEA SALT

1½ POUNDS BONELESS, SKINLESS CHICKEN BREASTS,
    CUT INTO LONG STRIPS
½ RED ONION, SLICED ¼-INCH THICK AND SEPARATED
    INTO RINGS
2 RED BELL PEPPERS, CUT INTO THICK STRIPS

2 HEADS BUTTER LETTUCE, SEPARATED INTO LEAVES
GUACAMOLE (PAGE 112)
SALSA (PAGE 49)

1. In a bowl, combine all the ingredients and whisk together until well incorporated.

2. Put the chicken in a medium bowl. Put the onion and peppers in a separate bowl. Pour half of the marinade over the chicken strips and the other half over the vegetables. Stir to combine. Marinate at room temperature for 20 minutes (or in the refrigerator for up to 8 hours).

3. Preheat a cast-iron skillet over high heat. When the pan is very hot, add the chicken and its marinade, searing on all sides until golden and cooked

through, about 3 minutes. Transfer to a heated serving plate. Let the pan get very hot before adding the vegetables and their marinade. Sear until the vegetables are hot, about 2 minutes.

4. Serve immediately with lettuce cups, guacamole, and salsa to make the fajitas at the table.

Meatloaf

Make an extra meatloaf to have on hand for sandwiches. To have the firmest slices, put a weight on top of the meatloaf. Put the meatloaf on a dish and top it with another dish holding one or two cans of tuna.

2 TABLESPOONS OLIVE OIL

½ ONION, MINCED

2 GARLIC CLOVES, MINCED

½ RED BELL PEPPER, MINCED

1 POUND GRASS-FED GROUND BEEF

1 POUND GROUND TURKEY

2 EGGS, BEATEN

¼ CUP ALMOND FLOUR

1 TEASPOON CHOPPED OREGANO

1 TEASPOON CHILI POWDER

½ TEASPOON CAYENNE PEPPER

1 TEASPOON SEA SALT

ONE 10-OUNCE PACKAGE FROZEN SPINACH, THAWED
    AND SQUEEZED DRY

½ CUP BARBECUE SAUCE (PAGE 121) OR PLUM SAUCE (PAGE 66)

1. Preheat the oven to 350°F.

2. In a skillet over medium-high heat, heat the oil. Add the onion and garlic and sauté until softened, 3 to 4 minutes. Add the pepper and sauté until softened, 3 to 4 minutes. Transfer to a large mixing bowl and let the mixture cool.

3. Add to the vegetables in the bowl the beef, turkey, eggs, almond flour, oregano, chili powder, cayenne, and salt. Mix until well blended. Fold in the chopped spinach.

4. Pack the mixture into a loaf pan or make a free-form loaf in a baking pan. Glaze the top of the loaf with barbecue or plum sauce.

5. Bake until the meatloaf is completely cooked (165°F), 50 to 60 minutes. Let the meatloaf rest for 10 minutes before slicing and serving.

Curried Pork with Apple and Squash

MAKES 4 SERVINGS

To keep the pork tender and flavorful, cook it until it is just done. Chicken breast or turkey tenderloins can be used instead of pork.

2 TABLESPOONS OLIVE OIL

4 BONELESS LOIN PORK CHOPS, TRIMMED

SEA SALT

FRESHLY GROUND BLACK PEPPER

1 ONION, THINLY SLICED

1 GARLIC CLOVE, MINCED

1 RED BELL PEPPER, CUT INTO THIN STRIPS

2 TEASPOONS CURRY POWDER

½ TEASPOON GROUND CUMIN

½ TEASPOON GROUND CINNAMON

½ CUP COCONUT MILK (FULL-FAT)

½ CUP BONE BROTH (PAGE 52) OR PREPARED CHICKEN BROTH

1 TART COOKING APPLE (SUCH AS GRANNY SMITH), CORED AND DICED

1 CUP CUBED, COOKED SQUASH

CHOPPED PARSLEY OR CILANTRO, FOR GARNISH

1. Preheat the oven to 350°F.

2. In a skillet over medium-high heat, heat the oil. Add the pork chops and cook until golden brown on both sides, about 6 minutes. Transfer the pork chops to a baking dish and season with salt and pepper.

3. Return the pan to medium heat. Add the onion, garlic, bell pepper, curry powder, cumin, and cinnamon, and sauté, stirring frequently, until the bell pepper is tender, about 4 minutes. Add the coconut milk and broth and bring to a boil. Add the apple and squash and pour the vegetable mixture over the pork.

4. Bake the pork until cooked through (145°F), 20 to 25 minutes. Serve the pork on heated plates topped with the vegetables and sauce.

CHAPTER SEVEN KID-FRIENDLY DESSERTS

Kid-Friendly Desserts

Dessert is an indulgence, but it serves an important purpose too. Having something sweet sends signals to the brain to help it recognize that the stomach is full. Many cultures enjoy fresh fruit at the end of a meal, an excellent practice. Some fruits like apples and pears can also be roasted, with or without a stuffing of nuts and dried fruit.

Life is full of reasons to celebrate with a special treat. In this chapter, you will find dessert recipes for holiday dinners and birthday parties, as well for the weekly cookie jar, now full of Paleo-friendly sweets.

Chocolate Chip Cookies

MAKES 2 DOZEN COOKIES

Almond flour tends to spread a little more than wheat flour and gives a wonderful crisp texture to cookies.

COOKING SPRAY (OPTIONAL)
3 CUPS ALMOND FLOUR
1 TEASPOON BAKING SODA
1 TEASPOON SALT
1 TEASPOON VANILLA EXTRACT
½ CUP VIRGIN COCONUT OIL, UNREFINED
½ CUP PURE MAPLE SYRUP
2 EGGS
1½ CUPS DARK CHOCOLATE CHIPS

1. Preheat the oven to 350°F. Line two baking sheets with parchment paper or spray with cooking oil.

2. In a bowl, combine the almond flour, baking soda, and salt.

3. In a separate bowl, blend the vanilla, coconut oil, maple syrup, and eggs. Add the wet ingredients to the dry ingredients and stir to make a smooth, heavy batter. Stir in the chocolate chips.

4. Drop the batter by the tablespoonful onto the baking sheets, leaving about 2 inches between each cookie.

5. Bake until the edges are browned and the cookies are set, about 15 minutes. Remove to a baking rack to cool.

Brownies

MAKES 12 BROWNIES

These brownies are dense and fudgy, with a subtle almond flavor and chunks of dark chocolate. Add dried fruits if you like; cherries and raisins are delicious.

COOKING SPRAY
½ CUP COCOA POWDER
1 TEASPOON BAKING SODA
½ TEASPOON SEA SALT
ONE 16-OUNCE JAR CREAMY, ROASTED ALMOND BUTTER
1¼ CUPS AGAVE NECTAR OR HONEY
2 EGGS
1 TABLESPOON VANILLA EXTRACT
1 CUP DARK CHOCOLATE CHUNKS

1. Preheat the oven to 350°F. Spray a 9-inch square baking pan with cooking oil.

2. In a mixing bowl, combine the cocoa powder, baking soda, and salt.

3. In a separate bowl, blend the almond butter, agave nectar, eggs, and vanilla. Add the wet ingredients to the dry ingredients and stir to form a smooth, heavy batter. Stir in the chocolate chunks.

4. Spread the batter in the prepared baking pan. Bake until the edges are browned and the center is set, about 25 minutes. Let cool on a baking rack before cutting into squares.

Carrot Cake

MAKES 1 CAKE

This cake is moist and light, more like an angel food cake than more famil-iar carrot cakes made with grated carrots and pineapple. If you are trying to revamp some of your family's favorite desserts, this is a perfect place to begin. The almond or coconut flour adds a subtle flavor to the cake. Serve it topped with fresh or stewed fruits, or a dollop of whipped coconut cream.

COOKING SPRAY

6 EGGS, SEPARATED

1½ CUPS DICED CARROTS, STEAMED UNTIL TENDER AND PURÉED

½ CUP RAW HONEY

1 TABLESPOON GRATED ORANGE ZEST

1 TABLESPOON FROZEN ORANGE JUICE

3 CUPS ALMOND FLOUR OR COCONUT FLOUR

1. Preheat the oven to 325°F. Spray a 9-inch round cake pan with cooking oil.

2. In a bowl, combine the egg yolks, carrots, honey, orange zest, and orange juice, and stir until combined. Add the almond flour and stir to form a moist batter.

3. In a separate bowl, whip the egg whites to stiff peaks. Fold the egg whites into the batter in two additions.

4. Pour the batter into the prepared cake pan. Bake until the edges are browned and the cake is set, about 50 minutes. Let cool completely on a baking rack. Serve in slices.

Triple-Berry Cobbler

This is perfect in the summer when berries are in season, but it is also wonderful in the winter when made with unsweetened frozen berries.

COOKING SPRAY

4 CUPS MIXED FRESH OR FROZEN BERRIES

1½ CUPS ALMOND FLOUR

2 TABLESPOONS COCONUT OIL, MELTED

2 TABLESPOONS HONEY

½ TEASPOON GROUND CINNAMON

1. Preheat oven to 375°F. Spray an 8-inch square baking dish with cooking spray.

2. Place the berries in the dish in an even layer.

3. In a bowl, combine the almond flour, coconut oil, honey, and cinnamon, and toss together until the mixture forms small crumbs. Scatter over the berries in an even layer.

4. Bake the cobbler until the topping is crisp and golden brown, and the juices are bubbly and hot, about 30 minutes. Serve hot or warm.

Pie Crust

MAKES ONE 10-INCH CRUST

This dough is fragile, so instead of rolling it with a rolling pin, you press it gently into place in the pie pan.

2 CUPS ALMOND FLOUR
¼ TEASPOON SEA SALT
2 TABLESPOONS COCONUT OIL
1 EGG, LIGHTLY BEATEN

In a bowl, combine the almond flour, salt, coconut oil, and egg. Using a fork, stir until the mixture resembles a coarse meal. Pour into a pie pan and press with your fingers in an even layer across the bottom and up the sides. Use immediately or chill in the refrigerator.

Pumpkin Pie

MAKES ONE 10-INCH PIE

This pie is a holiday star, but is equally delicious in any season. Choose puréed pumpkin that has no additions like sweeteners or flavoring.

ONE 15-OUNCE CAN PURE PUMPKIN PURÉE

3 EGGS

½ CUP COCONUT MILK

⅓ CUP RAW HONEY

1 TEASPOON GROUND CINNAMON

½ TEASPOON GROUND NUTMEG

⅛ TEASPOON GROUND CLOVES

1 UNBAKED PALEO PIE CRUST (PAGE 140)

1. In a bowl, combine the pumpkin, eggs, coconut milk, honey, cinnamon, nutmeg, and cloves, and whisk until smooth.

2. Pour the pumpkin mixture into the pie crust and bake until the custard is set and the crust is golden brown, 45 to 55 minutes.

3. Let the pie cool for at least 30 minutes before slicing and serving.

Ginger Apple Crisp

MAKES ONE 9-BY-13-INCH DISH

This popular dessert is perfect for weekday dinners as well as winter holidays and feasts, and it can do double duty as a warm, filling breakfast. Make more than you need for dinner, then warm it up the next morning. Try this with pears, peaches, or nectarines when they are in season, or use unsweetened frozen fruit when the season is over.

COOKING SPRAY

8 CUPS SLICED MCINTOSH OR GALA APPLES, PEELED, CORED, AND SLICED

½ CUP ALMOND FLOUR

½ CUP CHOPPED PECANS

2 TABLESPOONS FLAX MEAL

2 TABLESPOONS COCONUT OIL, MELTED

2 TABLESPOONS RAW HONEY

1 TABLESPOON GROUND CINNAMON

1 TABLESPOON GROUND GINGER

1 TABLESPOON VANILLA EXTRACT

¼ TEASPOON SEA SALT

1. Preheat the oven to 350°F. Spray a 9-by-13-inch baking dish with cooking spray. Place the apples in an even layer in the baking dish.

2. In a bowl, combine the almond flour, pecans, flax meal, coconut oil, honey, cinnamon, ginger, vanilla, and salt, and toss together until the mixture forms small crumbs. Scatter over the apples in an even layer.

3. Bake until the topping is crisp and golden brown and the apples are tender, about 45 minutes. Serve hot or warm.

Chocolate Banana Pudding

MAKES 4 SERVINGS

Making coconut cream is easy as long as you always have a can of full-fat coconut milk sitting in the refrigerator. You can use canned coconut cream, but you must find a brand that doesn't contain added sweeteners.

ONE 14-OUNCE CAN FULL-FAT COCONUT MILK, CHILLED
    IN THE REFRIGERATOR FOR AT LEAST 6 HOURS
1 RIPE BANANA
¼ CUP RAW HONEY
2 TABLESPOONS UNSWEETENED COCOA POWDER, PLUS
    EXTRA FOR GARNISH
1 TEASPOON VANILLA EXTRACT

1. Remove the coconut milk from the refrigerator and scoop out the solidified cream (save the remaining milk to use in other dishes). Using an electric mixer, whip the coconut cream until smooth and light.

2. In a bowl, mash together the banana, honey, cocoa, and vanilla and fold in the coconut cream. Spoon into pudding dishes and chill for at least 2 hours before serving.

3. Dust with a little cocoa powder before serving.

Paleo Substitutes

INSTEAD OF	USE
Baking powder	A combination of baking soda and an acidic ingredient (cream of tartar, lemon juice, molasses)
Bread, tortillas, and wraps	Lettuce or kale leaves, sliced meats, Paleo crêpes or wrappers
Butter	Coconut oil, lard, duck fat, ghee*, or clarified butter**
Cheese	Nut cheeses (vegan cheese substitutes may be suitable)
Cow's milk	Nut or seed milk (almond, coconut, hemp, cashew, etc.)
Deli meats	Gluten-free, nitrate-free brands
Granola and granola bars with oats	Granola and granola bars with nuts, seeds, dried fruits
Honey and syrups	Raw honey, Grade B maple syrup, agave syrup
Hot and cold breakfast cereals	Seed and nut-meal porridges (with fruit and vegetable purées and eggs), Paleo-friendly granola topped with nut milk
Mayonnaise	Homemade mayonnaise or a brand that is made only with oil, eggs, and seasonings; avocado
Peanut butter	Nut or seed butters
Pizza crust	Cauliflower purée or vegetable cakes (frittatas)
Sandwich bread or buns	Lettuce or kale leaves, sliced meats, Paleo crêpes or wrappers
Soy sauce	Coconut aminos
Sugar	Date sugar, palm sugar, coconut sugar, Sucanat
Wheat (and other grain) flours	Almond flour (made from blanched almonds), coconut flour, arrowroot flour, tapioca flour
Wheat pasta and noodles	Vegetable noodles, spaghetti squash noodles, prepared noodles made from a vegetable base
Whipped cream	Whipped coconut cream
White potatoes	Sweet potatoes, pumpkin, or hard squashes
White rice	Grated cauliflower
Yogurt	Coconut milk yogurt (made with grass-fed gelatin)

*Ghee is made by cooking butter long enough for the milk solids to separate from the rest of the butter. As it heats, it takes on a brown color and a nutty aroma and flavor before the butterfat is separated from the milk solids and water.

**Clarified butter is made by heating butter long enough to separate the milk solids and water from the butterfat. Only the butterfat is used; the water and milk solids are discarded. Clarified butter has a higher smoking point than whole butter and contains very little lactose, making it appropriate for some Paleo diets.

Kid-Friendly,
Paleo-Friendly Snacks

IF YOU WANT A SNACK THAT IS	TRY
Crunchy and savory (potato or corn chips, pretzels, tortillas, puffs and doodles, crackers, peanuts, popcorn)	Trail mix Cauliflower "popcorn" Vegetable chips from leafy greens, mushrooms, and other vegetables Vegetable "fries" Seed crackers or flatbreads Meat jerky
Savory but creamy and rich (cheese spreads, peanut butter, bean dips and spreads)	Nut "cheese" with fresh vegetables Avocado (mashed or sliced) or guacamole Nut butters (stuffed in apples or spread on celery) Paleo hummus made with vegetable purée and tahini Dips made with nut "cheese" or Paleo-friendly mayonnaise Hard-cooked or deviled eggs Smoked or canned fish (salmon, anchovy, herring, sardine, trout)
Frozen and sweet (ice cream, gelato, sherbet, or parfaits)	Fruit pops made with fruit purées or fruit and coconut milk Frozen coconut milk or cream Frozen puddings or pops made with fruits and coconut cream Churned "ice cream" made with nut milks and creams or fruit purées, and sweetened with Paleo-friendly sweeteners
Sweet (cookies, cupcakes, candy bars, cakes, pies)	Dried fruits, especially dates Dark chocolate (possibly melted for fondue with fresh fruit) Paleo-friendly granola bars, cookies, muffins, or doughnuts Nut-based cakes and pastries
Sweet and creamy (custards, mousse, creams, puddings)	Cooked puddings made with fruit purées or nut milks Mousse made with whipped egg whites and whipped coconut cream
Hot and spicy (flavored chips)	Beef jerky Salsas Gluten-free hot sauce (made with chiles, vinegar, and salt only) Prosciutto- or bacon-wrapped vegetables or dates, broiled

Index

Made in the USA
San Bernardino, CA
12 December 2018